K I N D E R G A

Learning Centers

Written by Bonnie Compton Hanson

Illustrated by Mark Mason

Cover Illustrated by Judy Hierstein

A Division of Frank Schaffer Publications, Inc.
23740 Hawthorne Blvd., Torrance, CA 90505

Table of Contents

To Teachers and Parents

Children love to learn—and they eagerly reach out to do so with all five senses. This makes learning centers the perfect medium to use to help kindergarten-age children learn some very valuable skills and some important Bible stories, too.

What is a learning center? A learning center is something your home or classroom is probably already full of, even if you never called it that. For instance, when you help your child roll out dough in your kitchen, that area of your countertop or table is an instant learning center. If you have a shelf or two of books or puzzles for the children to use, or a corner or table for blocks or playing house, these are learning centers as well.

This book is filled with a wonderful variety of crafts, games, prayers, snack ideas, songs, and other exciting activities children can do. The activities are designed to be set up in centers, and complete and easy-to-follow instructions are provided to help you easily set up a stimulating variety of learning centers, all based on well-loved Bible stories. Any necessary patterns have also been included.

There are 23 chapters featured in this book, each based on a Bible story from the Old or New Testament, and each containing wonderful ideas for a number of learning centers. Some of the learning centers featured in each chapter include these: pictures, books, puzzles and games, music, playhouse, art, blocks, nature, sand and water, active play, math and writing.

On pages 4–6 are brief descriptions of each of the centers mentioned above. Use these descriptions to implement any of your own ideas for learning center activities in addition to the ones provided in each chapter of this book. Also, be sure to read the featured Bible story in each chapter to the children and discuss it in detail with them before you begin the activities that correlate with it.

Learning Centers for Kindergartners

Some Basics About Learning Centers

All materials in a learning center should be as safe to use as possible. Even so, keep a first-aid kit, paper towels, and tissues handy. Any chairs should be sturdy and not easily tipped. Keep areas clean. If a sink or bathroom is not very close, have a way to clean up areas (and children) after messy art projects and before snacks.

Kinds of Learning Centers

Pictures Center

Pictures can help the children remember Bible stories and prepare them for reading. Use a bulletin board, an easel, classroom walls, or a low table to display any related pictures. You may wish to change your pictures by the week, month, or lesson. Large, beautiful Bible pictures can be ordered from Christian bookstores and publishers. If filed away when not needed, they can last for years. You can also include pictures the children have colored or figures cut from magazines. The children can help you put up the pictures.

Books Center

Looking at and listening to picture books is an essential part of learning to read. Provide the children with a wide variety of both library-bound and paperback picture books about Bible stories, nature, and other nonfiction books, especially those designed to teach skills and Scriptural values. Keep them on a low table or bookshelf. Let the children look through them at a table or on a story rug. Small, soft pillows are also nice. Keep your classroom Bible storybook in a special place and encourage the children to handle it very carefully. Sit on the rug with the children or in a story chair to read to small groups.

Puzzles and Games Center

Puzzles and other games are excellent for eye-hand coordination, matching skills, and visual discrimination. Many feature Bible stories and God's creation, and some are delightfully shaped.

Music Center

Music is a great way for children to learn Biblical concepts and helps children develop rhythm, tonal discrimination, and ear-body coordination. Pianos, guitars, zithers, xylophones, and electronic keyboards are great for kindergartners. Cassette players also make wonderful "teaching assistants," and take up a lot less room. Also include a set of rhythm instruments, purchased or handmade. There are many excellent songbooks and cassette tapes available for this age; you will find several songs in this book directly correlating with the lessons.

Playhouse Center

This dramatic play center can be as simple as some dolls, toy dishes, and a box of dress-up clothes. Or, you can have child-size stoves, sinks, refrigerators, tables and chairs, doctor and nurse kits, and dollhouses with figures and furniture. This is a great place for the children to try out grown-up roles and for socialized interaction. You may wish to keep some old pillowcases and towels in the dress-up box the children can use to create Bible-time costumes (along with old ties or strips of bright cloth for sashes).

Art Center

You may only have room for a table and chairs here, but if possible, also have at least one easel and a place for paintings to dry. This center stimulates the eye-skills of color and form, as well as tactile ones (with fingerpainting, play dough, etc.). Here the children can work with white and colored paper and newsprint, crayons, paints (poster and finger), markers, safe scissors, tape, glue, craft sticks, paste, clay, play dough, and other art materials—plus protective aprons or old shirts, if possible. Keep all supplies readily available, or set out each day's materials. Besides special projects, you may wish to keep a supply of coloring pictures, connect-the-dot pictures, and other activity pages handy for the children to work on.

Blocks Center

Every child loves to build with blocks. Wooden, plastic, and cardboard box-type blocks can all be used. Also, keep plastic toy animals and small toy cars, buses, trains, trucks, etc., here the children can use with the "houses" and "roads." Using blocks in a group situation requires not only small-muscle manipulation, but social and teamwork skills as well. So you will need to set up rules for this area concerning the "hogging" of blocks and floor space, taking blocks another child is using, and smashing someone else's work. You might enjoy having a specially designed "play rug" for this area that already has roads, houses, bridges, etc., printed on it.

Active Play Center

Areas for large-muscle, active play can be located either indoors or out, or both (especially in colder locations). Indoors, they would include equipment (purchased or homemade) for climbing on and through, as well as mats for rolling and tumbling. Outdoors, they can include swings, slides, tricycles, wagons, etc. If space is very limited, full-class games, such as tossing sponge balls or beanbags through hoops, and action rhymes can be organized and taught.

Nature (Science) Center

This center is an integral part of learning about God's wonderful world and how to care for it. A classroom occupied every day will want to have at least one live animal for the children to love and care for (rabbits are great), as long as it can be properly cared for on the weekends. Classrooms used only on one or two days a week can still have displays of rocks and pebbles, butterflies, flowers, bugs (non-pest type!), ant farms, flowers or other plants, colorful leaves, and aids such as magnifying glasses and magnets. Even in a city, the whole outdoors can be part of your nature center as you take nature walks around your church or school grounds.

Math and Writing Center

Although this center will probably not be included in most Sunday morning programs, it is essential for weekday kindergarten classes. Number and counting books and cards, sheets of reproduced number activities and pencils, balance scales, math activity boxes, and things to count are an integral part of this center. Letters to copy, word tubs with clearly printed words, and pre-reading workbooks and sheets should also be included.

Sand and Water Center

Children love sand and water! Both of these materials can be educational and messy, so close supervision is needed, especially for Sunday morning groups when children are all dressed up. You may use professionally made sand tables and water tables, or plastic tubs (about 12" x 18" x 6") that are easy for children to put their hands into. Be sure they are on a sturdy foundation. You don't have to keep these centers available at all times, but they are very handy for some lessons. Keep plastic containers, strainers, shovels, pails, and small toy boats nearby.

Other Learning Centers

Some classrooms, especially those used for weekday classes, may also have one or more of the following: Carpentry Center (for use with wood), Computer Center (including learning games), Listening Center (apart from the Music Center). Only the more common learning centers mentioned previously are featured in this book.

God Creates Our World

(Based on Genesis 1:1–10, 14–19)

In the beginning God created the heavens and the earth. (Genesis 1:1)

Children already know that the world about them is wonderful. This chapter provides the perfect opportunity to share with them the good news that their Heavenly Father created this world for them to enjoy! Help them delight in God's creation and thank Him for it.

Nature Center

Check These Out!

Materials needed: magnifying glass, rocks, pebbles, shallow pan of water

Directions: Display some small rocks and pebbles, or take the children on a nature walk and let them collect some of their own (they can even include small pieces of asphalt and concrete). Let the children examine them with a magnifying glass. Encourage the children to close their eyes and feel the rocks with their hands. Point out that some rocks are smooth, and some are rough, but God made them all. Let the children place the rocks and pebbles in water to see how different they look when wet.

Star Light

Materials needed: flashlight, piece of black plastic, rubber band

Directions: Punch small holes in the plastic and place it over the end of a flashlight. Hold it in place with the rubber band. Let the children turn on the flashlight and shine it into a dark corner to see the "stars" shine. Tell them that God created the real sun, moon, and stars to give us light.

Sand Center

Place plastic under the sand table or do this activity outdoors. Let the children add a little water to the sand (or do it for them). Let them make mountains, valleys, rivers, etc.

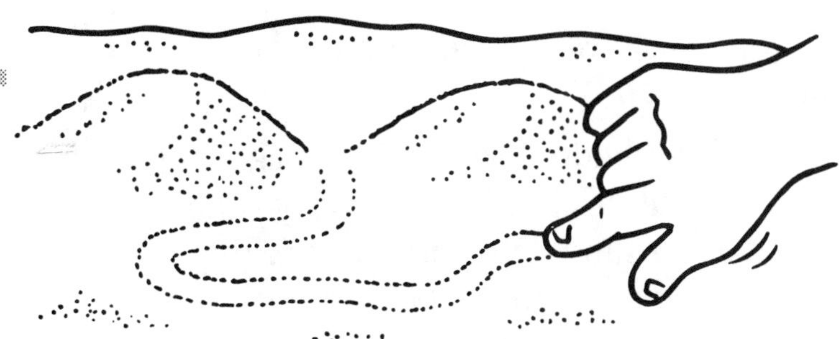

God Creates Our World

continued

Blocks Center

The children can pretend to build "mountains" with the blocks.

Music Center

God Made the World

Children will enjoy listening to ocean sounds in shells or on tapes. Let them sing the song below and do the motions.

(Tune: "Down at the Station")

God made the world	*(Point up, then make a circle with arms.)*
And everything I see.	*(Spread arms wide, then point to eyes.)*
The sun, moon, and stars,	*(Make a circle with arms, then a half circle with one arm, then make fingers "twinkle.")*
As lovely as can be.	
He made the mountains,	*(Make pointed triangle with arms and hands.)*
The oceans, and the sand.	*(Make "waves" with hands.)*
Thank You, God!	*(Point up.)*
The world You made is grand!	*(Clap.)*

Active Play Center

Catch the Sun

Materials needed: small, soft ball; piano or cassette music

Directions: Have the children sit in a circle. Tell them to pass the "hot sun" (ball) around while the music plays. Stop the music. See who is caught holding the sun. This child must tell one thing he or she likes about the sun. Discuss with the children the many wonderful qualities of the sun.

Art Center

Rock and Rolls

Materials needed: play dough or clay (optional: sand)

Directions: Children can make "rocks and pebbles" out of play dough or clay (and then roll them in sand). Be sure to print the children's names on the bottom.

God Creates Our World

continued

A Sky Full of Stars

Materials needed: one sheet of black paper per child, copies of the star and moon patterns on page 10, yellow crayons, scissors, glue (optional: glitter)

Directions: Instruct the children to color the stars and moon and cut them out. Then they can glue them onto the black paper (night sky). If desired, let the children put glue on the stars, and then add glitter. Be sure the pictures are dry before the children take them home.

Fun With Waves

Materials needed: blue finger paint, large sheets of newsprint (optional: pictures of oceans or lakes)

Directions: Discuss the wonder of oceans and lakes with the children. Give each child a large sheet of newsprint and some paint. Encourage them to make wave motions with their hands as they move the paint across the paper.

Creation Diorama (Part 1)

Note: This project will be added to as the children complete the next two chapters.

Materials needed: large cardboard box (like the kind copier paper comes in); purple, brown, and blue paper or plastic (can be adhesive); copies of the star and sun patterns on page 10; scissors; crayons; glue (optional: pebbles)

Directions: Tell the children that God has given us a beautiful, wonderful world and they can make a diorama of it. Cut off one side of the box. Line three sides with blue paper for sky. Cut one edge of the purple paper in a seesaw pattern to represent jagged mountain peaks. Cover the lower half of the sky area with these "mountains." Cover the bottom of the box with brown paper for ground. Cut out a curving piece of blue paper for water and place it over the brown paper. Let the children cut out the star patterns and one sun pattern and color them. Glue them to the "sky." The children can glue pebbles around for rocks.

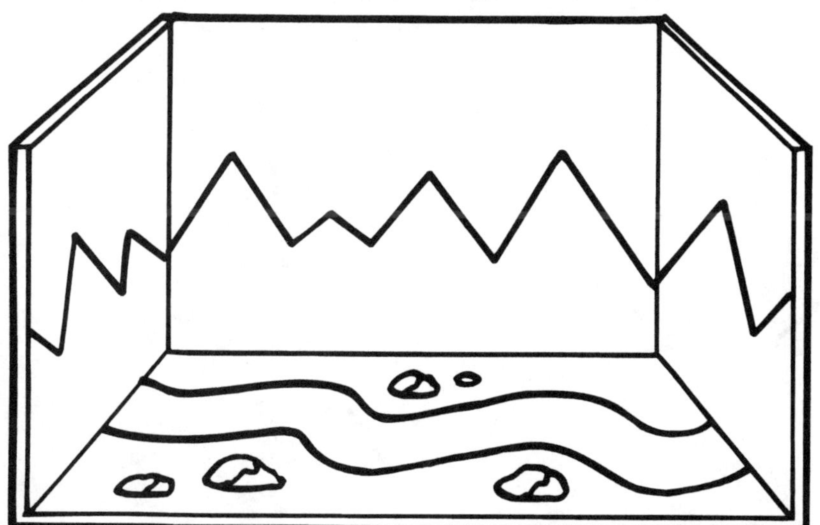

God Creates Our World

continued

Snack Time

Let the children enjoy small pieces of dry cereal and marshmallows in the shapes of stars, circles, etc. Or, let the children eat pieces of chocolate cookies for "land." Serve pretend "rain water."

Prayer: Thank You, dear God, for this wonderful world You made. In Jesus' name, Amen.

God Creates Plants and Animals

(Based on Genesis 1:1–11, 20–25)

He has made everything beautiful . . . (Ecclesiastes 3:11)

From the smallest blade of grass to the giant redwoods, from the wiggliest worm to the most majestic elephant—God made them all! This chapter provides a wonderful way to help the children appreciate the miracle of God's gifts of butterflies, dandelions, birds, their own pets, and their need to help care for these precious things God created.

Nature Center

If possible, take the children outside to look at and/or collect wildflowers, weeds, leaves, and insects. Put their "discoveries" on display. Or, let the children bring their own pets, insects, potted plants, etc., to make a display. Encourage the children to tell as much about each one as they can. Discuss the best ways to care for each. Let the children look at the plants and insects through a magnifying glass. Emphasize that each plant and animal, no matter how small, is a living creation and should be handled with care.

Playhouse Center

Children may take turns playing "animal doctor" to stuffed animals. Or, some may pretend to be kittens or puppies that the rest of the children care for. Tell the children to remember that God wants us to take care of the pets He gives us. Discuss with them what we should give our pets to eat and drink. Ask them how we can show them we love them.

Blocks Center

Let the children pretend to build a zoo out of large blocks and stuffed animals. Tell them that God loves His animals and wants them to have plenty of room to live in.

God Creates Plants . . .

continued

Active Play Center

Let's Be Birds (Action Play)

It's spring! It's spring! (*Clap hands.*)
We're birdies. Let's sing! (*Point to mouth.*)
Flap your wings on your nest, (*Flap arms.*)
Then fold them and rest. (*Put arms to side.*)
Now it's summer! Let's fly (*Flap arms.*)
Through the warm summer sky.
And when we're hot as can be, (*Wipe brow.*)
We'll fly down to a tree. (*Flap arms; move them downward.*)
Now it's fall. Trees are bare. (*Hold up hands with fingers separated like branches.*)
And it's cold in the air. (*Shiver.*)
So we fly off and sing, (*Flap arms.*)
"We'll be back in the spring!"

Kangaroo Hops

Place large soft blocks or books, about two feet apart, in a circle. As each child takes his or her turn, put an apron or old shirt with a large pocket for a "pouch" on the child. Put a small doll or stuffed animal in the "pouch" and encourage the child to jump over all the obstacles in the circle like a kangaroo. Ask the children if they are glad that God gives mother kangaroos a safe place to keep their babies in when they're jumping.

Art Center

Creation Mural

Materials needed: copies of the bird and leaf patterns on page 14; white, gold, or green background paper; paste; scissors; crayons or markers

Directions: For a spring and summer creation mural, use a green background and make a border of green leaves. For fall, use a gold background with red and yellow leaves. For winter, use a white background and no leaves. Print "God cares for His plants and animals" on the board. Let the children color and cut out the bird and leaf patterns. They can then paste these on the mural.

God Creates Plants . . .

continued

Creation Diorama (Part 2)

Materials needed: magazines, twigs, small plants, glue, scissors

Directions: Let the children add to the dioramas they began on page 9. They can add small pictures of animals and trees they cut from the magazines or draw themselves. They can also add real twigs for trees. Discuss how empty our world would be without plants and animals.

Music Center

Awesome Elephants

Children may sit, stand, or walk slowly in a circle as they sing the song below. Show the children how to hang their arms down in front of them with their hands folded together to create elephant trunks. They can also place open hands behind their ears for elephant ears. Help the children follow the actions.

(Tune: "Lazy Mary, Won't You Get Up?")

Elephants hang their trunks down low,
Their trunks down low, their trunks down low.
Elephants hang their trunks down low,
Swinging them as they go-oh!

Elephants throw their trunks up high,
Their trunks up high, their trunks up high.
Elephants throw their trunks up high,
Reaching right up to the sky-oh!

Elephants move their ears around,
Ears around, ears around.
Elephants move their ears around
So they can catch each sound-oh!

God helps them swing their trunks that way,
Trunks that way, trunks that way.
God helps them swing their trunks that way.
"Thank You, God!" I say-oh!

God Creates Plants . . .

continued

Snack Time

Stick animal crackers upright in pieces of celery spread with cream cheese or peanut butter (make sure no children are allergic!). Serve fruit juice. Remind the children that most of our food comes from the plants God gives us.

Prayer: Thank You, dear God, for the delicious food You give us and for the pets we love. In Jesus' name, Amen.

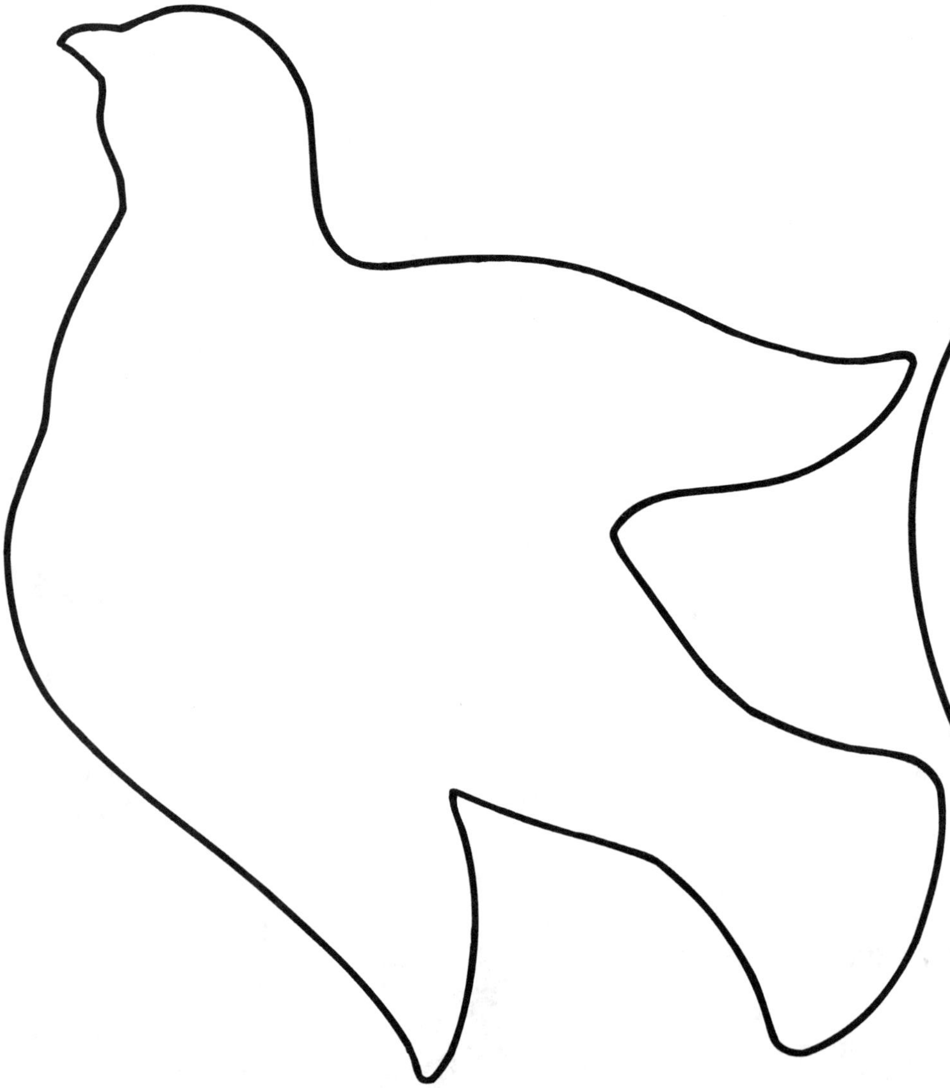

God Creates People

(Based on Genesis 1:26–2:25; 4:1–2)

Children, obey your parents in the Lord . . . (Ephesians 6:1)

God created a beautiful world. But He wanted something more: people to know and love Him. Children love learning about the world's first human family. Help them to be thankful to God for the families God has given them and to want to show love to both their families and to God.

Playhouse Center

The Very First Family

Children may pretend to be the first family. Daddy Adam is a farmer. He can use play gardening tools. Mommy Eve helps Adam and cares for their home and two little boys, Cain and Abel. Other children may play the family's sheep. The children can pray together to thank God for helping them.

Nature Center

Helping Adam Grow a Garden

Materials needed: small clay or plastic pots or planting trays, seeds for fast-sprouting flowers or grass, soil, small watering can

Directions: Ahead of time, put some soil in each pot or planting tray. Let the children put their own seeds in the soil. Show them how to add enough (but not too much) water. Set them out on a windowsill or table. If you won't be back in the room for several days, take the pots home with you for more watering, then bring them back to class. Tell the children that God is the one who will help the flowers pop up out of the ground and grow. But He wants us to help Him take care of them, just as He asked Adam and Eve to take care of the garden He created and everything in it.

Blocks Center

A Home for Adam

Have the children build a "house" for Adam and Eve and their children. If they want to add a garage or TV, let them know that people didn't have cars and TVs back then.

God Creates People

continued

Games Center

How Many?

Encourage the children to count with you as they play this counting game.

How many people were there at first?
This many. Nobody! NONE! (*Hold up closed fist.*)
Then God created Adam.
So now there was ONE! (*Hold up one finger.*)
Then God created Eve,
So now there were TWO! (*Hold up two fingers.*)
That's the same number
As me and you. (*Point to self, then to a child.*)
Then little baby Cain
Joined the family.
One and one make two.
One more makes THREE! (*Hold up three fingers.*)
"Thank You, God," said Eve,
"But we'd like one baby more."
God gave them baby Abel,
And then there were FOUR! (*Hold up four fingers.*)
Thank You, God! (*Put hands together in prayer.*)

Art Center

Baby Portraits

Materials needed: one copy of page 18 per child, crayons, pencils (optional: scraps of cloth; yarn; ribbon, including pink and blue)

Directions: After the children connect the dots, let them color and complete their pictures to create "portraits" of how they think they looked as babies. (Optional: The children can add cloth, yarn, and ribbon scraps to hair and clothes. Roll up each picture and tie it with a blue or pink ribbon.)

God Creates People

continued

Creation Diorama (Part 3)

Materials needed: small figures of a man, a woman, and two little boys cut from a magazine or catalog and glued to cardboard, or figures from a dollhouse

Directions: Using the diorama they began on page 9, the children can move the figures around to retell the Bible story of Adam and Eve.

Active Play Center

Down to a Crawl

Materials needed: real or toy baby bottle

Directions: Taking turns at being Adam, Eve, and baby Cain, the children can crawl on their knees on a safe surface (such as grass, carpet, or floor) from Daddy Adam to Mommy Eve (about eight feet apart), pick up a baby bottle, crawl back with it, and say, "Goo-goo, ga-ga."

Music Center

Families Are to Love

Be sensitive to the fact that not all children come from traditional, two-parent families. These children need their families' love just as much as those children from traditional families—maybe more. Teach the children the song below.

(Tune: "Jesus Loves Me")

I love my folks. They love me.
We're a happy family.
Fam'lies come from God above
To care for us and give us love.

Chorus:
I love my family, I love my family,
I love my family, and they all love me, too!

Prayer: Thank You, dear God, for our families who love us, and for the good food they give us every single day. In Jesus' name, Amen.

God Creates People

continued

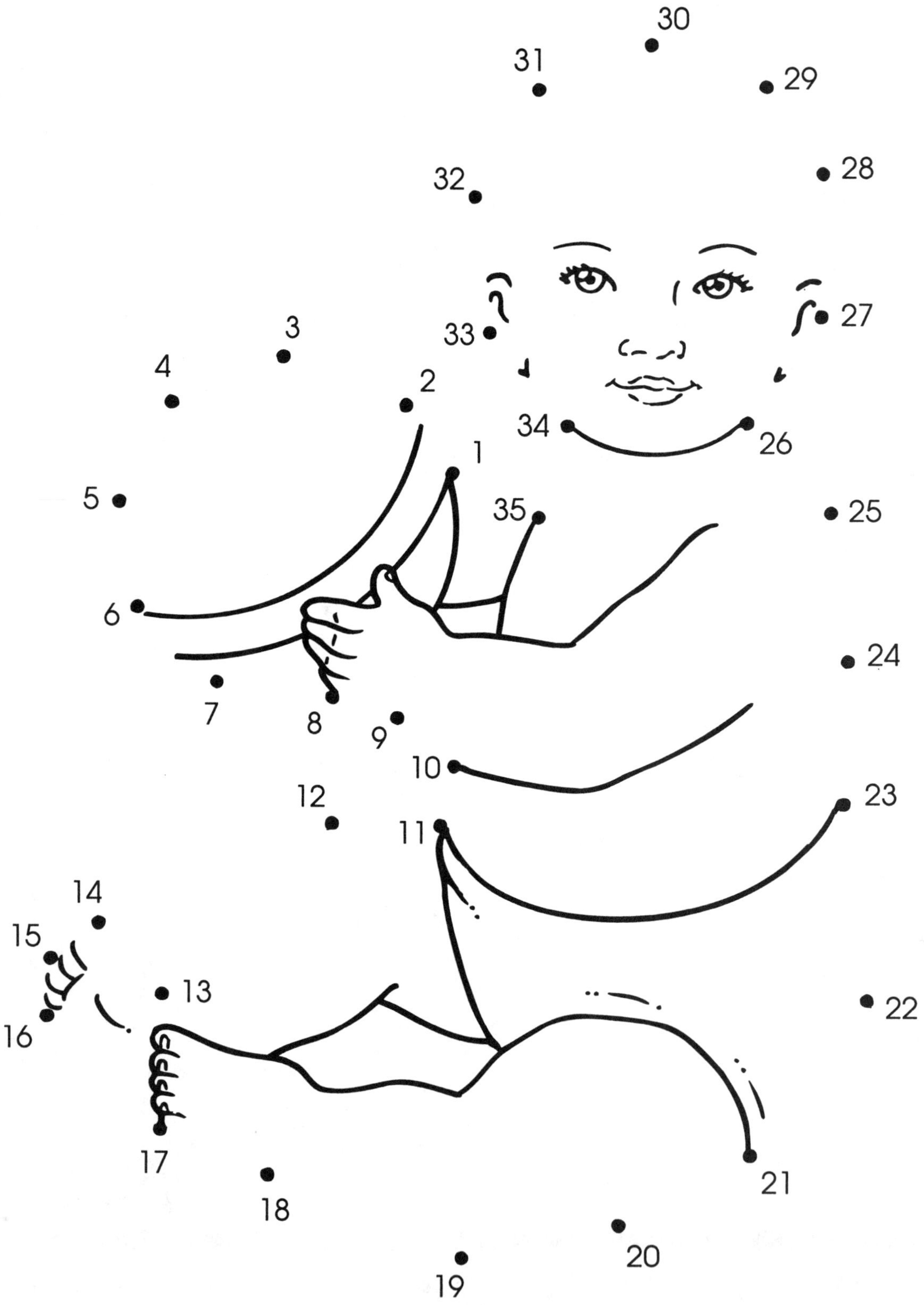

"I'm glad God gave me my family!"

God Keeps Noah Safe

(Based on Genesis 6:1–9:17)

The Lord . . . said to Noah, "Go into the ark . . ." (Genesis 7:1)

God's heart was sad. He was sending a great flood on the earth, but He wanted to save Noah and his family. He wanted to save all the animals, too. So He told Noah to build a special boat big enough to hold two of each land animal. Tell your kindergartners that they, too, can trust in God's protection, even when they are scared.

Blocks Center

Building an Ark

Children can pretend to use rulers and hammers as they build an ark to house the animals. Remind them that some animals, like rabbits, are small, but others, like elephants, will take up a lot of room. Tell them that they need one big door in one side for the people and animals to use.

Playhouse Center

Feeding the Animals

Using stuffed animals, children can pretend to feed, pet, and care for the animals just as Noah and his family did.

Nature Center

Taking Hamsters for a Boat Ride

Discuss class pets of any type, bring one from home, or look through books about animals with the children. Talk about the food, water, and exercise they would need on the ark.

God's Beautiful Rainbow

Materials needed: prism, crayons, paper

Directions: Tell the children that after the great flood, God put His rainbow in the sky as a promise that there would never be such a great flood again. Then explain to them that all colors of light together make white. The raindrops of the rainbow help break up light into separate colors, just as a prism does. Let the children experiment with the prism and then draw their own rainbows.

God Keeps Noah Safe

continued

Active Play Center

Here We Go, Two by Two

Divide the children into pairs. If you have an odd number of children, appoint your own "assistant." Teach the children the action rhyme below.

Here we go, two by two,	(*Point to pairs.*)
Just as Noah and the animals do.	
Hold on tight to your partner's hand.	(*Reach out hand.*)
First, bend over. Next, you'll stand.	(*Bend; stand up straight.*)
Now take steps like a tiny ant,	(*Take tiny steps.*)
Then big steps like an elephant!	(*Take large steps.*)
Look! The ark is right ahead!	(*Point ahead.*)
Shuffle your feet and nod your head.	(*Shuffle feet, nod head.*)
Now we're at the door. It's tall and wide.	(*Reach arms up, then out.*)
God shuts the door once we're all inside!	(*Slap hands together.*)
I hear the rain falling from the sky,	(*Put hand to ear to listen.*)
But inside the ark, we're safe and dry!	(*Clap hands.*)

Music Center

Noah Built a Big Old Ark

While singing the song below, let the children think of as many animals to sing about as possible. Remind them that fish did not go into the ark; they didn't need to. Also, children should use the word "some" before each animal's name, since none went in alone.

(Tune:"Old MacDonald Had a Farm")

Noah built a big old ark. E-I-E-I-O.
And on this ark, he had some sheep. E-I-E-I-O.
With a "Baa, baa" here, and a "Baa, baa" there,
Here a "Baa," there a "Baa," everywhere a "Baa, baa."
Noah built a big old ark. E-I-E-I-O.

Games Center

What Fits Where?

Put out some Noah's Ark and other animal puzzles. Take two simple ones and mix these pieces together. Encourage a team to work together to put the right pieces in the right puzzles.

God Keeps Noah Safe

continued

Art Center

Two by Two

Materials needed: two copies of the patterns below and one copy of page 22 per child, crayons, pencils, scissors, glue, three 8 1/2" x 11" sheets of paper taped together per child (or a large piece of newsprint)

Directions: Have the children color and cut out the patterns. Then they can glue the ark, Noah, and the animals on their papers wherever they wish. Next, have them add the banner. If the children use a large piece of newsprint, they can also draw in grass, trees, and other animals (at least two of each).

Snack Time

Serve an "ark" snack of apple slices and raisins.

> *Prayer:* Thank You, dear God, for taking care of Noah and the animals, and for taking care of me, too. In Jesus' name, Amen.

God Keeps Noah Safe

continued

God kept the animals safe.

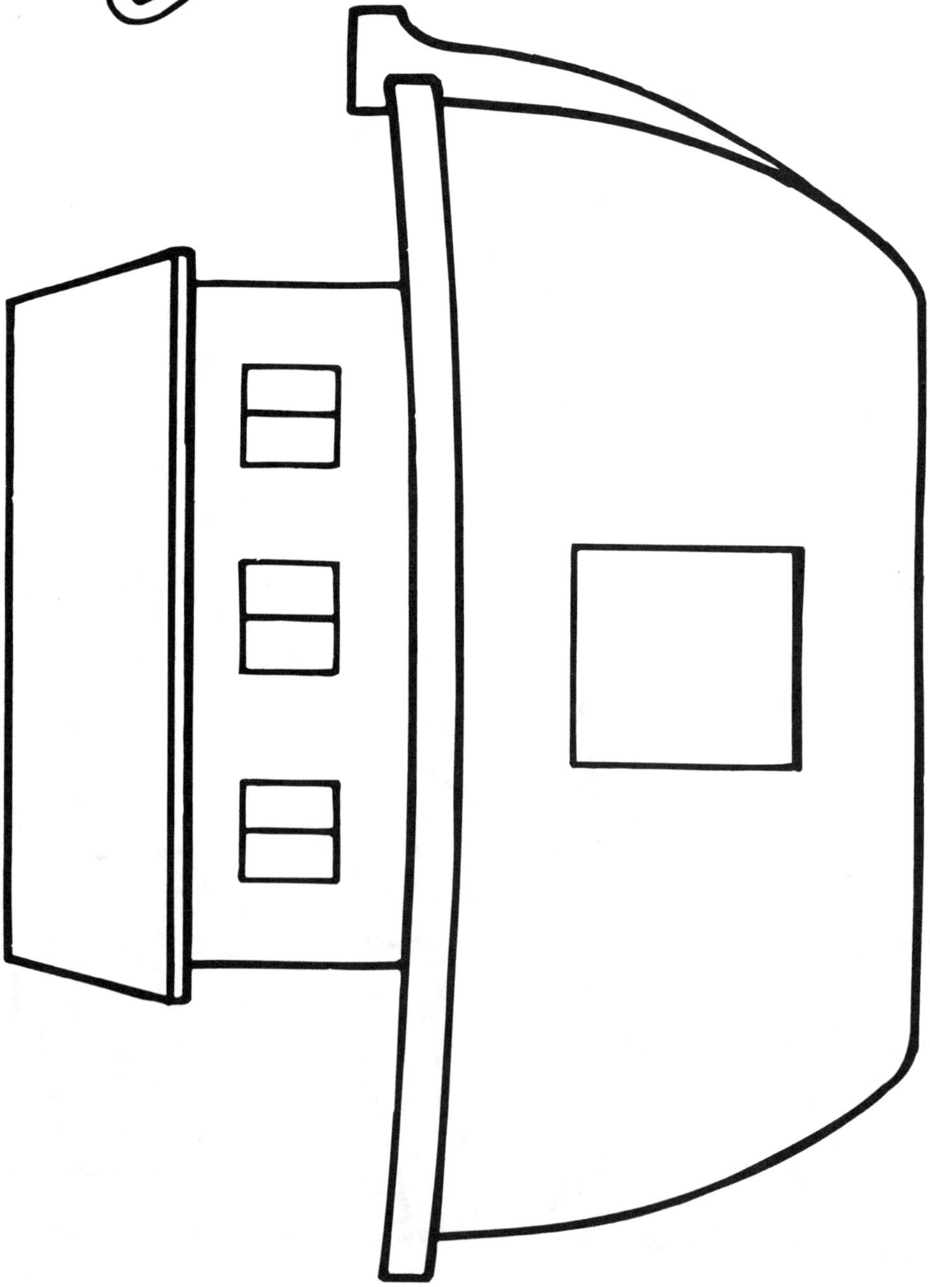

Sarah Laughs for Joy

(Based on Genesis 12, 15:1–21:7)

. . . the Lord said ". . . Sarah . . . will have a son" . . . (Genesis 18:10)

God promised Abraham and Sarah that He would give them a new home in a new land for their descendants. But years passed without children. When they were very old, God still made them that promise. Abraham and Sarah laughed. But finally, when Abraham was 100 and Sarah was 90, they became parents. They had a son whom they named Isaac. God always keeps His promises!

Playhouse Center

Caring for Baby Isaac

Children will enjoy caring for "babies" just as mother Sarah did. Using towels or clothes from a dress-up box, the children can also enjoy acting out the Bible story of Sarah, Abraham, and baby Isaac.

Music Center

A Laughing Song

This song is a perfect way to help the children remember the story of Abraham and Sarah.

(Tune: "London Bridge")

God once promised Abraham, Abraham, Abraham,
God once promised Abraham, "A son I will give to you."

But Abraham said, "Ha, ha, ha! Ha, ha, ha! Ha, ha, ha!"
Abraham said, "Ha, ha, ha! You don't mean that, do You?"

God then promised Sar-ar-ah, Sar-ar-ah, Sar-ar-ah,
God then promised Sar-ar-ah, "A son I will give to you."

But Sar-ar-ah said, "Ha, ha, ha! Ha, ha, ha! Ha, ha, ha!"
Sar-ar-ah said, "Ha, ha, ha! You don't mean that, do You?"

God kept all His promises, promises, promises,
God kept all His promises with Isaac, not long after.

His parents then said, "Ha, ha, ha! Ha, ha, ha! Ha, ha, ha!"
His parents then said, "Ha, ha, ha!" for Isaac's name means "laughter!"

Sarah Laughs for Joy

continued

Active Play Center

"Just Like Baby Isaac" (Action Play)

Our parents were glad to see us come,
Just like baby Isaac's. *(Hold arms; rock the baby.)*

We went "Goo-goo" and sucked our thumb,
Just like baby Isaac. *(Suck thumb.)*

We kicked our feet and bobbed our head,
Just like baby Isaac. *(Move feet and head.)*

"Thank You, God," our parents said,
Just like baby Isaac's! *(Put hands together to pray.)*

Games Center

The Giggle Game

Materials needed: beanbag or soft ball

Directions: Have the children form a circle. Explain how the game is played. To play, the children must keep passing the "giggle ball" or "giggle bag" from one to another until the leader suddenly says, "Stop!" Whoever is holding the ball or bag at that time has to laugh or giggle and then tell about something that makes him or her happy. Continue passing the ball for several turns. Tell the children that God is glad when we are happy and what can make us happiest of all is to love Him.

Nature Center

See How Much I Grew!

Materials needed: baby doll in a bed or bassinet, measuring tape or ruler, height chart or blank paper on a wall

Directions: Have a baby doll in one corner in a baby bed or bassinet. With a ruler or measuring tape, help the children compare a baby's height with their height. Mark their heights on a class wall chart.

Sarah Laughs for Joy

continued

Blocks Center

A Road to the New Land

After hearing about Abraham and Sarah's travels, the children may wish to build a road from their old city of Ur to their new land. Remind them that there were rivers to cross as well as mountains.

Art Center

A Year of God's Promises

Materials needed: large calendar, pen (optional: holiday stickers)

Directions: Select a large, colorful calendar, a Christian one if possible. Children can help you write in birthdays and other special events for the year. Special stickers for holidays and birthdays make it extra fun. Ask the children if they know that God promises to be with us and help us on every single one of these days. This makes a whole year full of His promises!

A-MAZEd at God's Promises

Materials needed: one copy of page 26 per child, pencils, crayons

Directions: Have the children start with Abraham and Sarah at Ur on the lower right and then work their way up to Haran and on to Canaan, where Isaac was born. After they complete the maze, tell them to color their picture.

Snack Time

For a truly "happy meal," serve cupcakes or cookies with yellow, smiling, frosting faces. For a happy drink, fill a glass jar or pitcher with lemonade or fruit drink and get it very cold. Then draw a smiling face in the condensation on the outside with your finger.

Prayer: Thank You, dear God, for giving baby Isaac to Abraham and Sarah to make them happy. Thank You for giving me my family, too. In Jesus' name, Amen.

Sarah Laughs for Joy

continued

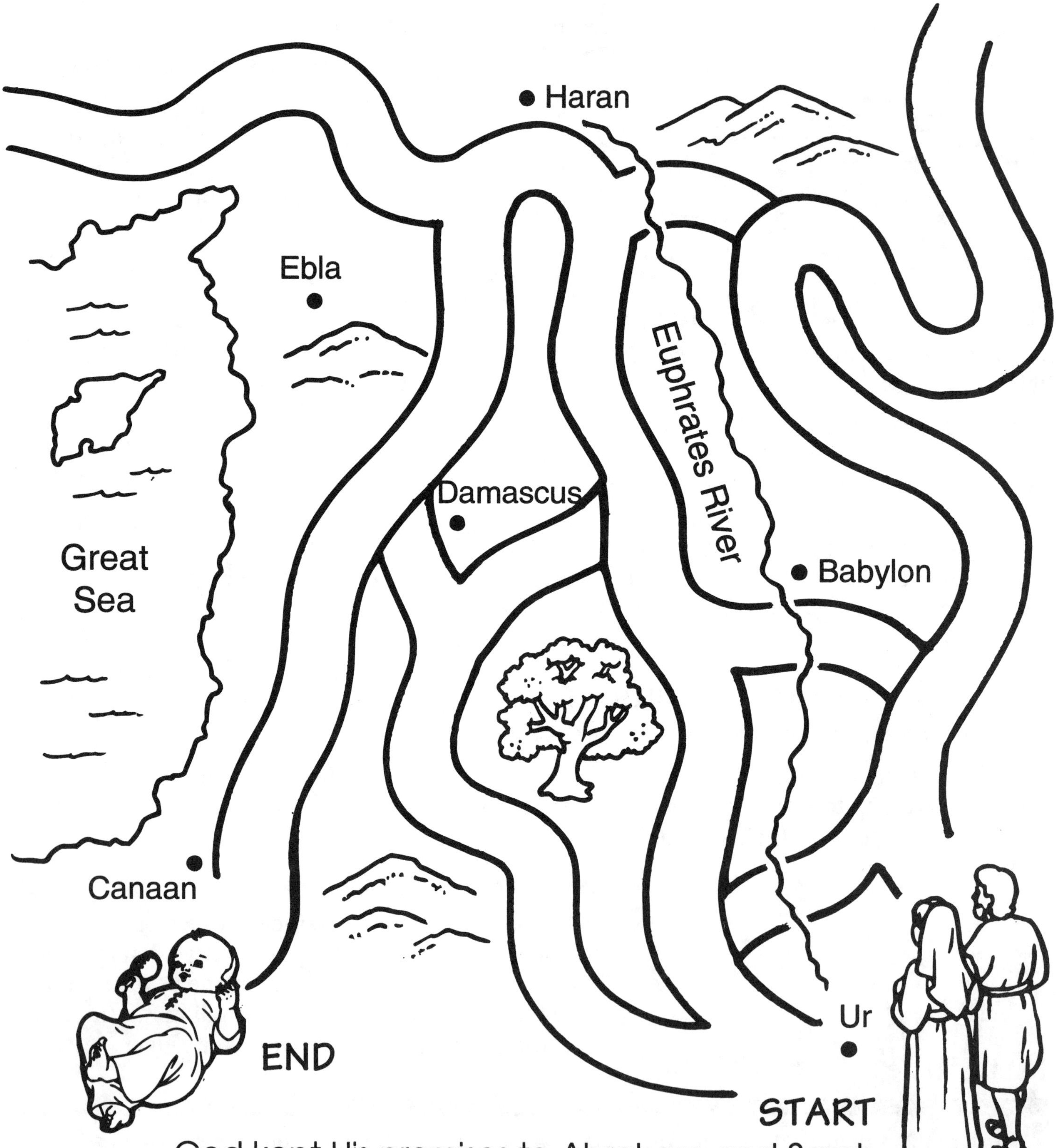

Haran

Ebla

Euphrates River

Damascus

Great Sea

Babylon

Canaan

Ur

END

START

God kept His promises to Abraham and Sarah.

. . . the Lord said ". . . Sarah . . . will have a son." . . . (Genesis 18:10)

Rebekah Helps a Stranger

(Based on Genesis 15:2; 24:1–51)

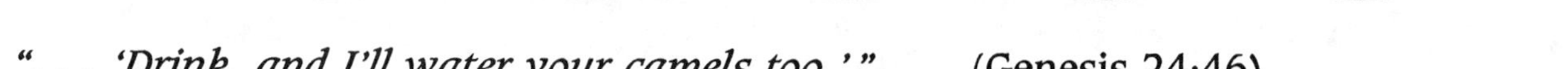

". . . 'Drink, and I'll water your camels too.' " . . . (Genesis 24:46)

When Isaac grew up, Abraham worried that he might marry a girl who didn't love God. So he sent his faithful servant off with 10 camels to the city where his relatives lived to seek a God-fearing wife for Isaac. The children will be thrilled that God not only helped Abraham's servant make the trip, but also meet at the village well the exact young woman he was looking for!

Art Center

Making a Jar for Rebekah

Materials needed: modeling clay or play dough

Directions: The children will enjoy molding simple bowls or pots. For a small one, roll a ball and push thumb firmly down through the top middle. The insides of larger balls can be scooped out. For a handle, roll a small, thin, round strip and attach it to the top and middle of one side. Make sure the handle is thick enough to stand up on its own. Some children may be skillful enough to roll long strips and spiral them around and around on top of each other to make the pot. Do not let the children actually drink from their pots.

The Missing Pot

Materials needed: one copy of page 29 per child, crayons, glue, scissors (optional: one copy of the jar silhouette on white paper and one copy of the puzzle pieces on colored paper per child)

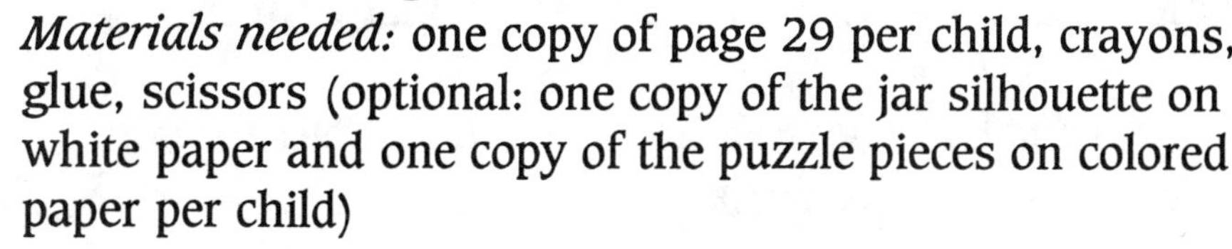

Directions: Help the children cut the page in half on the dotted lines. Then have them color and cut out the puzzle pieces and paste them on the jar silhouette. The children may color all the pieces the same, or they can make each one different.

Playhouse Center

Getting Ready for Company

Children will enjoy preparing a meal at Rebekah's house for Abraham's servant and his camels. Be sure to set out plenty of "water" for the camels to drink. They will also enjoy acting out this Bible story.

Rebekah Helps a Stranger

continued

Music Center

God Loves Me, Too!

(Tune: "Good Night, Ladies")

God loved Abraham, God loved Abraham,
God loved Abraham, and God loves me, too!

(Continue with "God loved Isaac, camels, Rebekah," etc.)

Active Play Center

"Humping Our Way Along" (Action Play)

"Good-bye, faithful camels," says Abraham. (*Wave good-bye.*)
"Please find Rebekah as fast as you can." (*Point and shake finger.*)
So off go we camels, humpety-hump, (*Move feet and put one hand on back like "hump."*)

Over the desert, clumpety-clump.
Now we go down to a valley so low. (*Lean over and place hands near floor.*)

Then up over mountains this high we must go. (*Stand up, reach arms high.*)
Stompety-stomp, we're walking some more. (*Move feet, show hump.*)
We're thirsty! We're tired! Our backs are too sore! (*Make a sad face. Rub back.*)
There's a nice place to rest, and a well, too, we think! (*Point.*)
Won't someone please give us some water to drink? (*Put hand to throat. Pretend to pant.*)

"Here, camels," says Rebekah, "is a drink just for you." (*Hold out jar.*)
So we drink and we drink and we DRINK till we're through. (*Pretend to drink.*)
Thank you, Rebekah! (*Clap.*)

Snack Time

Serve glistening squares of gelatin dessert made with mandarin orange slices, like the jewels and gold Abraham sent to Rebekah (or candy orange slices and gumdrops), with lots of water for hungry camels. Have the children help you serve the others, as Rebekah did.

Prayer: Thank You, dear God, for helping Rebekah be kind. Help me be kind, too. In Jesus' name, Amen.

Rebekah Helps a Stranger

continued

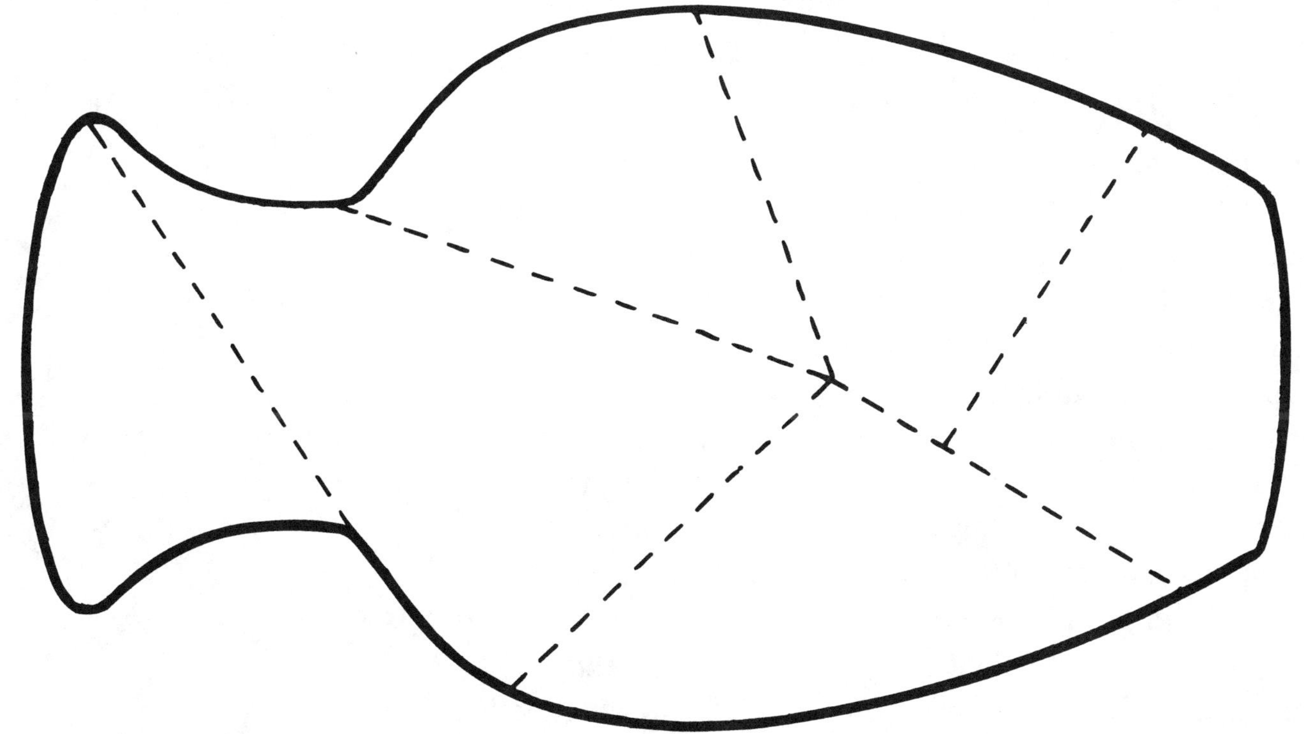

Jacob Dreams

(Based on Genesis 28:1–22)

. . . *"Surely the Lord is in this place . . ."* (Genesis 28:16)

Although Jacob was a grown man, he was leaving home for the first time and going far away to visit relatives he had never met. Worse, he had quarreled with his brother and been in trouble with his father. How lonely he felt away from his family! But when he camped for the night, God gave him a wonderful dream and told Jacob He was with him. What comfort to the children to know that God is always with them, even at night or far from home!

Playhouse Center

Let's Go Camping!

Children can make bedrolls to carry and then set up "campsites" and "cook" their dinner over a campfire as they act out this Bible story. Before lying down to "sleep," they can thank God for taking care of them.

Nature Center

Nature Walk

If weather permits, children can take a walk around outside, pretending to take a long journey as Jacob did. They can collect twigs for their "campfire" and perhaps take their snack along for a picnic (see "Snack Time," page 32).

Active Play Center

Jacob's Dream (Action Play)

Jacob's been walking all day long. (*Pretend to walk.*)
His legs are sore. His feet are sore. (*Rub one foot; make a face.*)
The sun's now setting in the west. (*Point.*)
He's far too tired to walk some more. (*Rub eyes.*)
So Jacob sits down on a rock. (*Sit down.*)
He rests his feet and looks around. (*Stretch out feet; look around.*)
He eats his dinner, then lies down. (*Pretend to eat, then lean head on hand or really lie down; close eyes.*)
And soon he's sleeping on the ground.
He has a dream! A stairway goes (*Point up.*)
Right up to heaven and God's throne! (*Point up.*)
"I'm with you, Jacob!" God tells him. (*Point up, then to others.*)
"You never have to be alone." (*Shake head.*)
Thank You, God! (*Put hands together for prayer.*)

Jacob Dreams

continued

Music Center

Children will enjoy listening to tapes of beautiful instrumental music by a harp or violin to remind them of the angels in Jacob's dream. Or, let them play wind chimes or a small xylophone. You could also sing "Climb, Climb Up Jacob's Ladder" or the song below.

Jacob's Dream

(Tune: "Row, Row, Row Your Boat")

Jacob had a dream, he had a dream one night,
Of a stairway up to heaven, glowing very bright.
Shining angels, too, were on every hand,
Going up and down the stairs, obeying God's command.
Then God said to him, "Do not worry so.
I will always be with you everywhere you go."
Jacob woke and said, "Surely God is here,
With Him always by my side, I've no need to fear!"

Blocks Center

Building a Stairway

Children will enjoy building stairs out of large blocks or boxes, inspired by the one in Jacob's dream. Explain to children that we know we can't really build a stairway to heaven, but we don't have to. God is right here with us to help us and show us His love.

Art Center

God Is Always With Me

Materials needed: pictures cut from magazines, newspapers, or catalogs of children doing different activities with adults, other children, or alone; glue; large piece of newsprint

Directions: Print "GOD IS ALWAYS WITH ME" across the top of the sheet of newsprint. Discuss with the children the situations depicted in the pictures. Ask the children if God is with us when we play ball, when we help Mom, when we sleep, when we go to church. Let the children glue the pictures on the mural.

Jacob Dreams

continued

Night Time for Jacob

Materials needed: one copy of page 33 per child, crayons (optional: scraps of flannel large enough to cover the picture of Jacob, star stickers or glitter and glue)

Directions: The children can draw a smile on Jacob's face and stars in the sky and then color their pictures. (Optional: Show the children how to cut out a piece of flannel for a blanket or a sleeping bag for Jacob. They could also add star stickers to the night sky instead of drawing them; or help the children add glitter to the ones they drew. The children could also draw Jacob's dream.)

Story Circle

Have the children gather in a circle around a "campfire" of real branches or pretend ones from Lincoln Logs®, Tinkertoys®, or other toy sticks.

Games Center

God Is Here; I've Nothing to Fear

Materials needed: handkerchief or other cloth to use as a blindfold

Directions: Have the children stand in a circle. One child, "Jacob," is blindfolded and stands in the center. Turn "Jacob" around a couple of times. Jacob says, "God is here." The other children reply, "I've nothing to fear." Then Jacob tries to find and tag one of the other children. If Jacob succeeds, blindfold the child that was tagged. If Jacob fails after two attempts, let another child have a turn anyway until all have tried.

Snack Time

Serve a picnic snack of trail mix (raisins, sunflower seeds, pieces of dried fruit) and small boxes of juice with built-in straws. If taking an indoor or outdoor hike first, the children can carry their lunches in plastic or paper bags.

Prayer: Thank You, dear God, for being with Jacob, and for always being with me, too. In Jesus' name, Amen.

Jacob Dreams

continued

God was with Jacob, and He's with me, too.

God Saves Baby Moses

(Based on Exodus 1:1–2:10)

. . . She named him Moses, saying, "I drew him out of the water." (Exodus 2:10)

What desperate times for God's people! Not only were they forced into bitter slavery, but the pharaoh had ordered all their boy babies to be killed. However, God worked through the faith and courage of a mother, the resourcefulness of a daughter, and the kindness of a princess to save a baby—not just any baby, but the one God planned to some day rescue all His people!

Nature Center

Helping Baby Moses Float

Materials needed: wide container of water, small empty plastic container with lid (like plastic egg, sandwich keeper, etc.), small plastic figure for baby Moses

Directions: You may try this outside with pans, tubs, or wading pools in warm weather. Otherwise, use pans or the sink inside. Let the children experiment with the water. Ask them why a leaf floats while a rock sinks. Let the children make waves with their hands. Ask them why there are bubbles in the water. (trapped air) Put the figure inside the container, close the lid, and set it on the water. Ask the children why baby Moses is all right. (There is air inside the container, but no water.) If you have a classroom aquarium, let the children watch and perhaps feed the fish.

Music Center

Let the children lie on a rug and pretend to swim as they listen to a tape with ocean sounds. Or, sing the song below with the children.

Itsy-Bitsy Moses

(Tune: "Itsy-Bitsy Spider")

Itsy-bitsy Moses' mother went to pray:
"Dear God, don't let them take my boy away."
God helped his mother make a basket then
For an itsy-bitsy boat to put the baby in.
Itsy-bitsy Moses' sister stood nearby.
Along came a princess. She heard the baby cry.
"Itsy-bitsy baby," she said, "we'll care for you."
Then itsy-bitsy Moses laughed, "Goo-goo-goo-goo-goo!"

God Saves Baby Moses

continued

Games Center

Fishing in the Nile

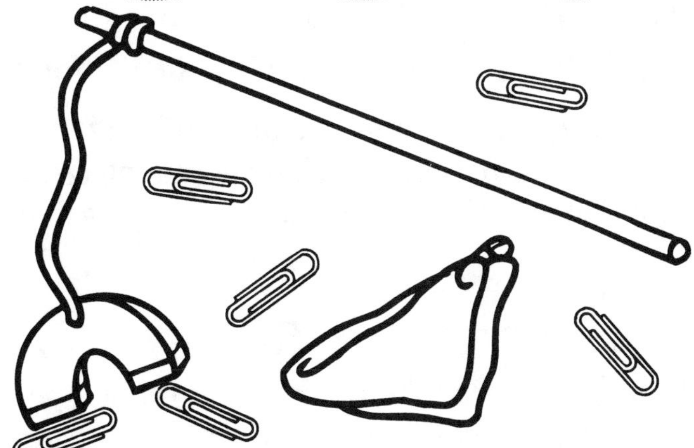

Materials needed: magnet with a hole in it; sturdy but not pointed stick or pole; string; small square of cloth or facial tissue; metal safety pin; chair or stool; several small, safe steel or iron objects (like other magnets or paper clips, but not nails)

Directions: Tie one end of the string to the stick; attach the magnet to the other end. Scatter the remaining steel objects on the floor. Fold the square of cloth or tissue diaper-style and pin it securely with the safety pin to represent baby Moses. Put "baby Moses" on the floor with the other objects. Let the children take turns sitting on the chair or stool, fishing in the "Nile River" for fish, catching as many as possible without touching and waking up baby Moses.

Active Play Center

Sleeping in a Basket (Action Play)

Moses' mother rocked her baby in her arm.	(*Join hands, rock arms.*)
"I'll put you in a basket," she said, "away from harm."	(*Keep rocking arms; nod head.*)
So Moses' mother put him in a basket boat,	(*Pretend to lift baby.*)
Then set it on the water, and watched the basket float.	(*Make "waves" with hands.*)
Miriam watched from nearby to see that he was OK.	(*Put hand over brow to watch.*)
Then suddenly she saw a princess come that way!	(*Look surprised.*)
Her ladies took the basket out. "Let's look at what's inside!"	(*Pretend to lift something from water.*)
And so they opened up the lid. Then baby Moses cried.	(*Pretend to open lid; cry.*)
"Poor baby!" said the princess. "We'll take good care of you."	(*Make kissing sounds.*)
That made Miriam happy, and baby Moses, too!	(*Clap.*)

Running to the River

Materials needed: two dolls, each in a bag or basket

Directions: If the children like to play team games, line them up into two teams. The first child in each team has a baby Moses in a bag or basket. Pick another point for the river—such as a tree or a chair. When you say "go," the first child in each team runs to the river with baby Moses and then back home, handing baby Moses to the next child. The first team with all players back "home" wins. If this game gets too boisterous, you may have the children tiptoe instead, so the pharaoh won't see baby Moses.

God Saves Baby Moses

continued

Blocks Center

Building a River

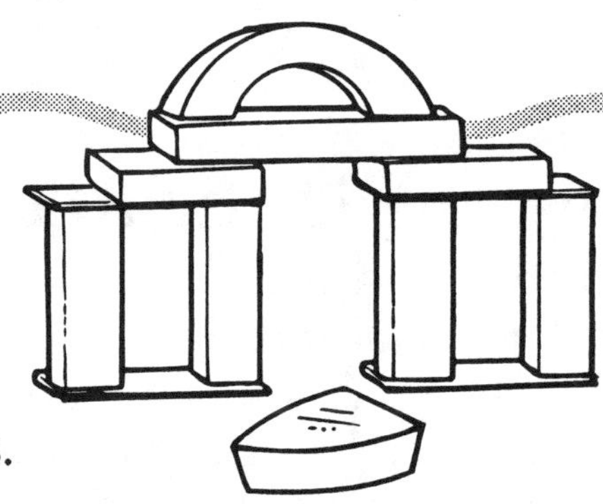

Materials needed: pictures of pyramids, toy boats

Directions: Children may enjoy building the Nile River with blocks and toy boats. Include a safe place along the shore for baby Moses. They may also build a palace nearby for the princess.

Art Center

Floating on the River

Materials needed: blue poster paint and sponge or finger paint, newsprint, one copy of page 37 per child, crayons, tape, scissors, glue (optional: several 6" pieces of green yarn per child)

Directions: With a sponge or fingers, let each child cover a sheet of newsprint with blue paint to resemble a river. Then the children can color and cut out their baby Moses pictures. When the paintings are dry, let the children glue baby Moses in the basket on it. Then the children can tape the basket covers on the top edge of baby Moses. They can also glue on "bulrushes" (wavy green yarn pieces). Make sure the children understand that baby Moses was near the shore where the water is shallow and plants can grow. *Instead of the painting activity, the children could also cut out the pictures and cover and glue them onto a piece of white or blue paper.

Playhouse Center

Let's Play Baby Moses!

Children will enjoy finding treasures from the dress-up chest to play the various characters in this Bible story—Moses' mother, Miriam, the princess, her ladies. Use a doll for baby Moses and a basket or shoebox to put it in. Designate one area as the "river." If the children are playing outside, the "river" can be a sandbox or a sidewalk. Help the children rejoice at God's loving care for baby Moses.

Snack Time

Serve fish crackers in a small basket along with a green fruit drink.

Prayer: Thank You, dear God, for taking care of all of us children, just as You took care of baby Moses. In Jesus' name, Amen.

God Saves Baby Moses

continued

Where can baby Moses hide? Open the cover and look inside.

Crossing the Sea

(Based on Exodus 7–14)

. . . the Israelites went through the sea on dry ground . . . (Exodus 14:22)

God had called Moses to lead His people out of Egypt, from slavery to freedom. He sent plagues to make the pharaoh let them go. Now the people were gathered at the edge of the Red Sea. Normally, they would have crossed along a well traveled road. But the pharaoh's army was chasing them. How could they get across? Your kindergartners will thrill at how wonderfully God solved the Israelites' problem.

Music Center

God's People Go Marching On

Let the children play the song below using rhythm instruments and tambourines as they listen to you sing. Then let them sing along with you. When they are familiar with the song, they can march around the room singing and playing, or they could even visit another classroom.

(Tune: "Battle Hymn of the Republic")

God's people stood upon the shore and they all sadly said,
"How can we cross the water? We will drown and all be dead."
But Moses said, "With God's help, we will all be safe instead.
Yes, God will help us through!"

Chorus: Glory, glory, halleluia! Glory, glory, halleluia!
Glory, glory, halleluia! God will help us through!

Pharaoh's army's coming, for he doesn't want them free.
But all night long, God blows His wind across the deep Red Sea.
When morning comes, He's made a path as dry as it can be.
God will help us through!

Chorus

The children look around them as the water piles up high,
But underneath their feet, the bottom of the sea is dry.
"Glory, halleluia!" all the happy children cry.
"God will help us through!"

Chorus

Blocks Center

Building Pyramids

The children may pretend to be Israelite slaves, building pyramids or other great buildings for the Egyptians, while they wait for God to free them.

Crossing the Sea

continued

Nature Center

Appreciating a Miracle

Materials needed: pan, pool, or sink of water; cloth or paper towels (optional: shells)

Directions: Let the children experiment pushing the water to each side with their hands. Ask them if it stays. Encourage them to blow on the water. That will move the water, but of course, it comes right back. Tell the children that only God has the power to make water stand straight up in the air and then stay there long enough for all of His people to cross over the sea. The children can also see what the shells looked like wet and then dry.

Playhouse Center

Moving Away

After dressing up from the dress-up chest, the children can pretend to pack up their belongings, eat their last (Passover) meal together, then set out (around the room) for the new home God is leading them to. Discuss the sad things about moving (leaving friends behind) and the happy ones (new friends, new home). Tell the children that even when we move to a new home, God is with us, and He takes care of us wherever we are. If the weather is good, the children can go outside for their walk.

Art Center

From Slaves to Free

Materials needed: one copy of page 41 per child, crayons, ruler, pencil

Directions: Give each child a copy of page 41. Show them how to fold the top left and right corners forward so that the flaps meet to make a pyramid. The children can then draw lines across the pyramid to make rows of stones. Have them color their pictures. Tell the children that their pictures represent the type of work God's people were forced to do. Tell the children to draw sad faces on the lower left and happy ones on the lower right to show how the Israelites felt when they were slaves and then how it felt to be free.

Crossing the Sea

continued

Active Play Center

Catching the Army

Materials needed: several very soft beanbags

Directions: Divide the children into two groups—pharaoh's army and the Israelites. Have pharaoh's army line up in two lines and throw "hard work" (the bags) at the Israelites, who run through the middle of the two lines. Next, the Israelites line up in two lines and pretend to be walls of water as they throw their bags at the army running through. Then the children can switch roles. On a hot day when the children are appropriately dressed, go outside and use damp or wet sponges instead of beanbags.

Crossing the Red Sea (Action Play)

God's people hurry down the road. Everybody's glad.	(*Move feet fast; smile.*)
They leave old Egypt far behind, the place that made them sad.	(*Point behind; look sad.*)
But what is this? There's water just as far as they can see!	(*Put hand over brow; look about.*)
There's no boat to cross it. And here comes a whole army!	(*Shake head; look shocked.*)
"God will help us," Moses says. He stretches out His hand,	(*Point up; stretch out hand.*)
And all night long, the water blows away at God's command.	(*Blow; move hands.*)
Next morning when the children wake, what do the children see?	(*Rub eyes.*)
Between two walls of water is a path dry as can be.	(*Reach arms high.*)
God's people all cross safe. Uh-oh! Now here come Pharaoh's men!	(*Clap, then look shocked.*)
Those walls of water fall, ker-splash! And they're never seen again!	(*Make a loud splash; clap.*)

Snack Time

Cut off the crust from bread and spread the slices with peanut butter, deviled ham, or other spread. Slice the bread diagonally. Stand up the triangles like pyramids. Serve with milk.

Prayer: Thank You, dear God, for helping Your people become free from that mean pharaoh. In Jesus' name, Amen.

Crossing the Sea

continued

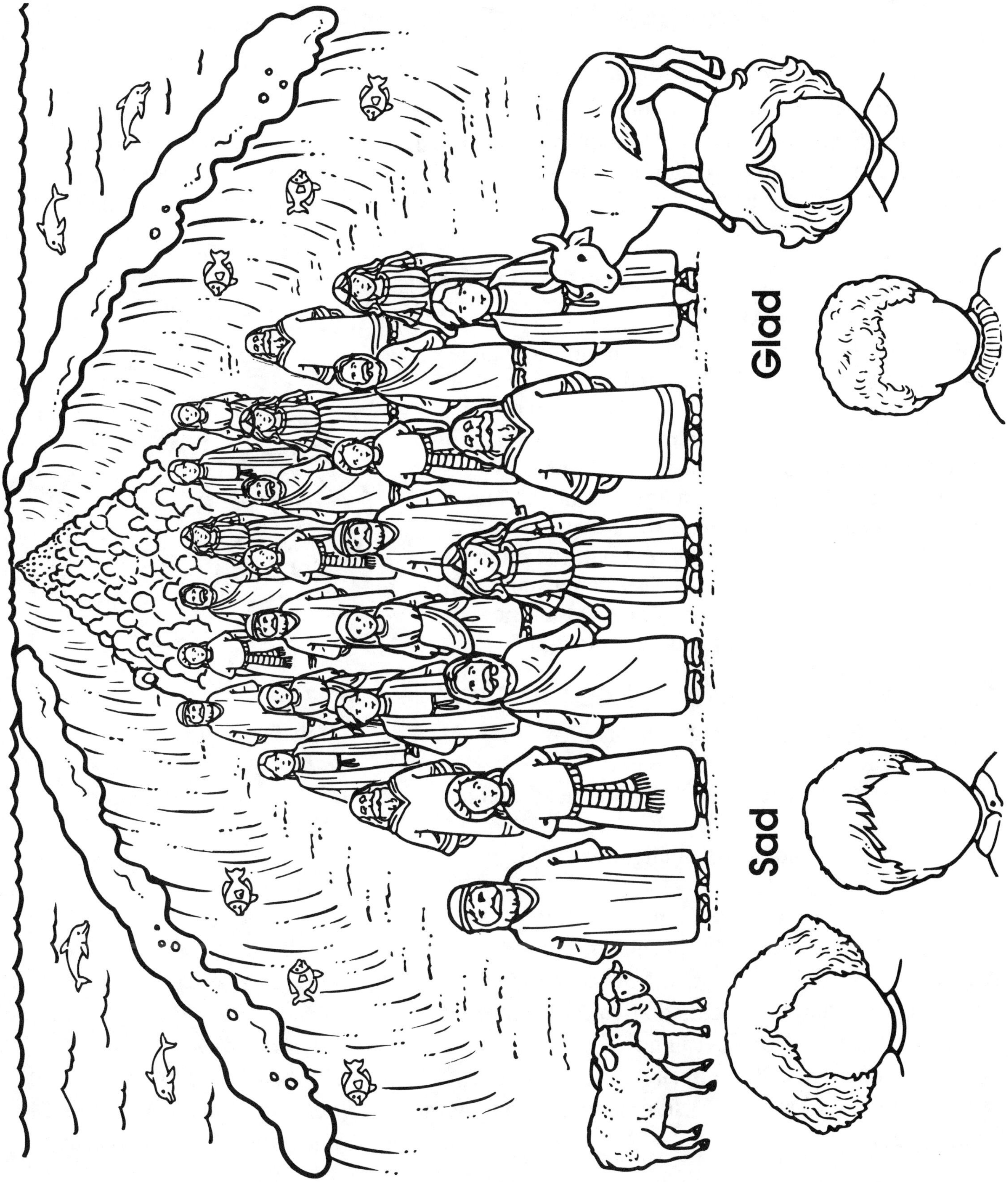

Glad

Sad

Samuel Hears God Call

(Based on 1 Samuel 3)

. . . *"Speak, for your servant is listening."* (1 Samuel 3:10)

Of course the children are aware that God talks to grownups, such as their parents and the pastor, but maybe they wonder if God talks to a mere child. This is one of the joyous wonders in this Bible story. Help the children understand that God talks to all of us through His precious Word. And be sure the children know that they talk to Him each and every time they pray.

Active Play Center

Who's That Calling?

Blindfold a child who is "It." Stand "It" in the middle of a circle and turn this child around a few times. Tell the child that it is dark. Ask him or her to try to tell who's calling to him or her. Point silently to someone in the circle, who then will call out (without screaming or whispering) the name, "Samuel." The child in the center tries to guess whose voice called to him or her. If the child can't figure it out, the other children can give hints, such as "Her name starts with a 'buh' sound" or "rhymes with Dan." Let all the children who wish to have turns at being "It."

"Samuel Wakes Up" (Action Play)

Let's be little Samuel, sleeping in his bed. *(Lie down or lean head on hands.)*

His blanket's to his chin, and a pillow's 'neath his head. *(Pull blanket to chin; pat pillow.)*

Suddenly, he hears someone calling, clear as day. *(Sit up straight; put hand to ear.)*

He runs to see old Eli. "Here I am!" he'll say. *(Move feet fast.)*
But Eli has been sleeping. "Did I call you? No! *(Rub eyes.)*
Why, it's the middle of the night. Now back to bed you go!" *(Move feet fast.)*
One, two, three times, he hears that voice, it's true. *(Hold up three fingers.)*
Finally, old Eli says, "God is calling you." *(Point up, then out.)*
Then next time God calls Samuel, he listens carefully. *(Put hand to ear.)*
How glad I am God wants to talk to kids like you and me! *(Point up, then to self.)*
Thank You, God! *(Put hands together to pray.)*

Samuel Hears God Call

continued

Music Center

Have the children lie on a rug with their eyes closed and listen to songs about prayer or the Bible (such as "The B-I-B-L-E"). Or, have them sing one or both of the songs below.

Are You Sleeping, Samuel?

(Tune: "Are You Sleeping?")

Are you sleeping, are you sleeping, Sam-u-el, Sam-u-el?
Somebody is calling, somebody is calling. Listen well, listen well.

"Did you call me, Pastor Eli?" Samuel said, Samuel said.
"No, I didn't call you," said Pastor Eli. "Go back to bed, back to bed."

Two more times then Samuel got up. Said Eli, said Eli,
"God's the one who's calling, God's the one who's calling.
Say 'Here am I,' say 'Here am I.'"

Each Time I Hear God's Word

(Tune: "Jingle Bells")

When God's Word's told to me, I listen carefully
Because I want to see what God wants me to be.
I know God's Word is true and tells me what to do.
And everything I hear God say, I'll listen and obey.

Chorus: I will hear, I will hear, everything You say.
Dear God, help me learn Your Word so that I can obey-ey!
I will hear, I will hear, everything You say.
Dear God, help me learn Your Word so that I can obey!

Playhouse Center

Moving Away

Children can use dress-up clothes and paper or plastic bags to help young Samuel pack up and move away from home. Ask the children what he will need in his new home. Ask them what toys he should take with him. Have the children walk around the room to "God's House." Or, they can stop by the story rug for a Bible story.

Samuel Hears God Call

continued

Blocks Center

Building God's House

Encourage the children to use blocks to build God's house for old Eli and young Samuel.

Art Center

My Bible Book

Materials needed: one copy of page 45 per child, crayons, pencils

Directions: Have the children fold their pages in half and then in half again along the fold lines to form a book. The children can trace the words on their book covers and then color them and the picture. On the last page, the children can write their names and draw pictures of their families. Children can take their books home to share with their families.

Game Center

Waking Up Samuel

Have the children crouch in a circle, putting their arms around their legs. Choose one child to be "It." Have "It" walk around the back of the circle and then touch a child on the head, thus "waking up Samuel." That child (Samuel) chases "It" around the circle. If "It" reaches the child's vacant spot before he or she can return, "Samuel" becomes "It."

Snack Time

Let the children feast with fresh grapes and chocolate chip cookies. Serve lemonade or milk.

Prayer: Thank You, dear God, for this food and for Your Book. In Jesus' name, Amen.

Samuel Hears God Call

continued

HOLY
BIBLE

My Name

"We love to look at our Bible Book."

God Helps David Win

(Based on 1 Samuel 16,17)

"The Lord . . . will deliver me . . ." (1 Samuel 17:37)

So often, children are considered second-rate citizens. Children realize there is so much they can't do. How thrilled they are when you help them learn to do more, to do better, to be better. And God wants to help them, too. This is one reason the timeless story of a brave young shepherd lad thrills them so much. What was impossible for David alone was possible with David and God together.

Music Center

David, the great psalmist and harpist not only wrote most of the psalms himself and organized great choirs and orchestras, but he has also inspired many musicians in the many years since. Children may wish to listen to harp music or the spiritual, "Little David, Play on Your Harp." Or, they can sing the song below.

David Was a Shepherd Boy

(Tune: "Jesus Loves Me")

David was a shepherd boy who played on his harp for joy.
All around the sheep would graze as he sang his psalms of praise.

Chorus: Yes, David loved God. Yes, David loved God.
Yes, David loved God. And God loved David, too.

Goliath was a giant tall. "I'll kill you all!" he told King Saul.
"No," said David, "God will be our protector—wait and see!"

Chorus

David took some stones he found—little pebbles, smooth and round.
He shot a pebble through the air. Goliath fell down, then and there!

Chorus

Everyone loved David then. He'd chased away Goliath's men.
But David said, "I'd rather sing praise to God than anything."

Chorus

Playhouse and Blocks Centers

Playing for a King

Let the children play palace. They can build a palace and a throne room. Then they can dress up and sing and play for King Saul as David did.

God Helps David Win

continued

Art Center

Making Harps to Play

Materials needed: one Styrofoam dinner plate cut in half per child, scissors, hole punch, yarn (optional: stickers or crayons)

Directions: Cut out the flat center of the plate, leaving only the curved rim. Punch three holes in the rim near one end and three at the other. Tie a piece of yarn firmly behind one hole; lace up and down for harp strings. Let the children decorate and play while singing or acting out this Bible story.

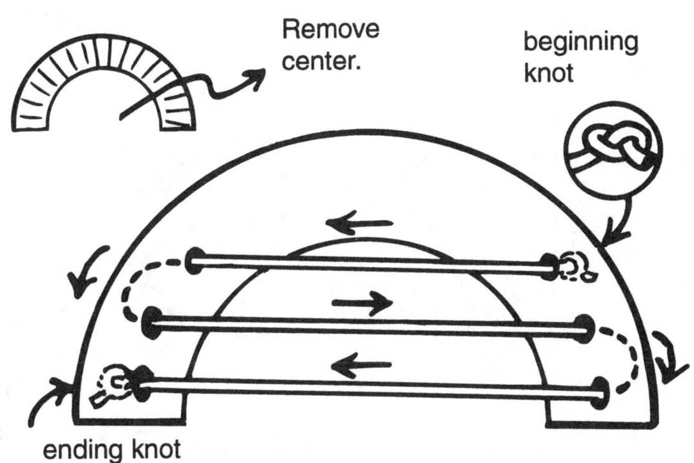

A Crown for King Saul

Materials needed: one Styrofoam dinner plate per child; scissors; metallic paint, or glue and glitter, or a strip of glittery Christmas garland

Directions: Help the children cut out the centers of the plates and decorate as desired to create crowns. The children can wear their crowns and pretend to be King Saul.

David and Sheep Mural

Materials needed: one extra David picture from page 49 for the class, one copy of page 49 per child, one yard of green cotton flannel, white flannel strips, cotton balls, glue, crayons, scissors

Directions: Fasten the green flannel securely to a wall or bulletin board. Cut out and color the extra David figure. Let the children color their patterns, cut them out, and write their names on the backs. Glue small strips of white flannel to the backs of all patterns. Have the children glue cotton balls to the front sides of their sheep. Put your David in the center of the green flannelboard. Let the children place one of their sheep on the board. They can take their other sheep and their David patterns home.

God Helps David Win

continued

Nature Center

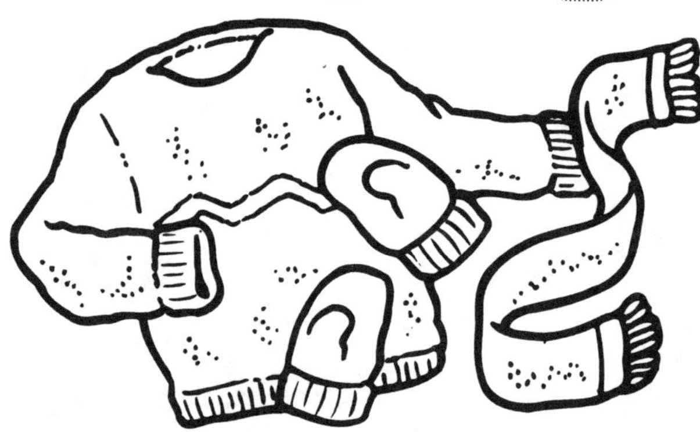

Materials needed: pictures of sheep; pieces of sheepskin and fur; wool scarf, mittens, sweater, or other clothing, plus clothing made from leather, silk, cotton

Directions: Discuss with the children what sheep eat. Let them shut their eyes and feel the difference between sheep's wool and regular fur, and between clothes made from wool and the other clothes.

Active Play Center

Getting Even With Goliath

Materials needed: beanbags, child-sized basketball hoop on a stand or a bucket on a chair

Directions: Tell the children to pretend the beanbags are pebbles. They can try to throw them into their target just as David threw his pebbles at Goliath.

Stopping the Bear

Have a starting point and an ending point. Tell the children that they are lambs. Hold up a little stuffed bear and say, "Fuzzy, fuzzy bear with fuzzy, fuzzy hair. You can't get me, so there, there, there!" Then all the lambs run away from the bear and race to the finish line.

David's Little Lamb (Action Play)

I'm a little lamb. I go, "Baa, baa, baa." (*Make sheep noises.*)
I like to run and play, and go "Ha, ha, ha!" (*Move feet; laugh.*)
But one day, I heard something. "Grr, grr, grr!"— (*Make a growling noise.*)
A big, mean bear with fur, fur, fur. (*Reach hands high to "measure;" make a face.*)

That bear headed right for me, me, me! (*Put hands over eyes; shiver.*)
"God will help," David said. "You'll see, see, see." (*Point up.*)
David grabbed that bear right there, there, there. (*Grab with hands.*)
And that was the end of that bear, bear, bear. (*Wipe hands against each other.*)
Then David set me down on his lap, lap, lap, (*Pretend to pet animal on lap.*)
And sang me to sleep for a nap, nap, nap! (*Put head on hands; close eyes; smile.*)

God Helps David Win

continued

Snack Time

Children will enjoy cupcakes or cookies with frosting and colored sprinkles on top. Let them make green ones for grassy pastures; white ones (or shredded coconut) for wooly sheep. Serve with cool lemonade like the cool water sheep like to drink.

Prayer: Thank You, dear God, for helping David. Help me to be brave for You, too. In Jesus' name, Amen.

Rebuilding the Wall

(Based on Nehemiah 1:1–6:16)

. . . the people worked with all their heart. (Nehemiah 4:6)

Nehemiah helped the people see that rebuilding Jerusalem's wall was important both for their own safety and for God's glory. The children will be thrilled to see what can be done through dedicated teamwork and dependence on God.

Nature Center

Materials needed: pieces of rock, concrete, and pebbles

Directions: Let the children handle the rock pieces, including scratching one rock against another to show how hard and strong rock is. Discuss why rock is a good material for building strong walls.

Music Center

These can be used as action songs. They are so simple that the children might sing them all.

Jerusalem's Wall Was Very Tall

(Tune: "Merrily We Roll Along")

Jerusalem's wall was very tall, very tall, very tall, *(Reach up on tiptoe.)*
Jerusalem's wall was very tall, till it had a fa-all. *(Bend over, putting hands to the floor.)*

Nehemiah came to say, came to say, came to say, *(Point finger.)*
Nehemiah came to say, "Let's rebuild the wa-all."
And so the people worked and worked, worked and worked, worked and worked,
And so the people worked and worked, everyo-one. *(Pretend to hammer.)*
Then the wall stood tall again, tall again, tall again, *(Reach up on tiptoe; clap.)*
Then the wall stood tall again when they were do-one.

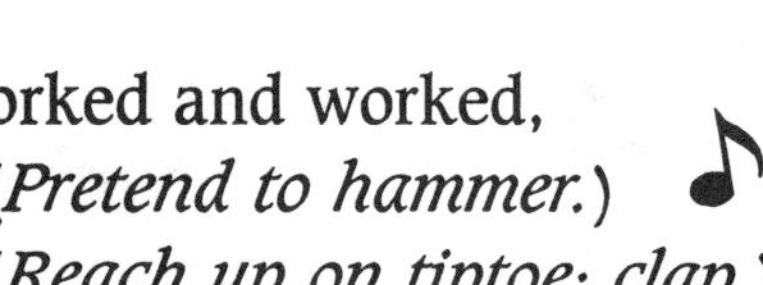

Hi-Ho, Jerusalem

(Tune: "Farmer in the Dell")

Jerusalem's wall was tall, Jerusalem's wall was tall.
Hi-ho-the dairy-o, Jerusalem's wall was tall.
And then it had a fall, and then it had a fall.
Hi-ho-the dairy-o, and then it had a fall.

Ideas for other verses:
We're building back the wall . . .
And now the wall is tall . . .

Rebuilding the Wall

continued

Nehemiah Built a Wall

(Tune: "Old MacDonald")

Nehemiah built a wall, E-I-E-I-O.
The people helped him build it tall, E-I-E-I-O.
With a hammer, hammer here, and a hammer, hammer there,
Here a hammer, there a hammer, everywhere a hammer, hammer,
Nehemiah built a wall, E-I-E-I-O.

Ideas for other verses: "with a dig, dig, lift, lift, saw, saw," etc.

Ten Little Walls

(Tune: "Ten Little Indians")

As you sing the first verse, point to various children to fall down or sit down.

One little, two little, three little walls,
Four little, five little, six little walls,
Seven little, eight little, nine little walls,
Ten little walls fell down.

Then point to various children to stand back up as you point and sing.

One little, two little, three little walls,
Four little, five little, six little walls,
Seven little, eight little, nine little walls,
Ten little walls back up.

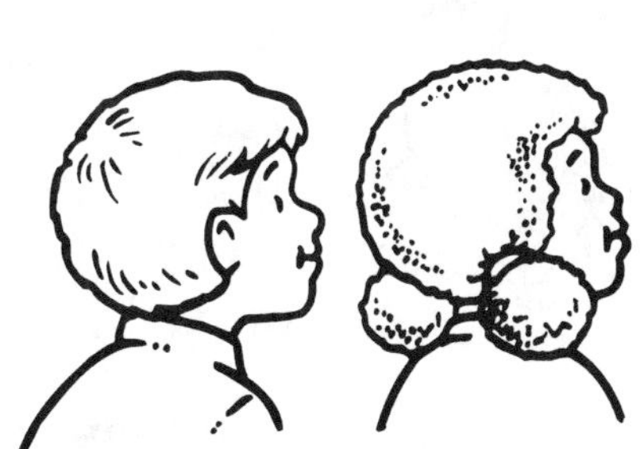

Art Center

Rejoicing in the Wall

Materials needed: one copy of page 53 per child, crayons, scissors

Directions: Have the children color the workers and fold the page in half on the fold line. Have the children color the top cover to look like a wall with a door on it. Then the children can lift up the door to see the happy workers.

Rebuilding the Wall

continued

Blocks, Playhouse, and Games Centers

Building a Strong Wall

The children can build a large wall either inside or outside. Remind them to leave at least one "gate" area open for people to go through. Then the children can dress up and celebrate their finished wall or act out the Bible story. Tell the children that people used to build walls around cities to keep out robbers and other enemies.

What's the Password?

Using the wall children make as described above, have two children stand at the gate as gatekeepers. In order for another child to go through, he or she must say a word that rhymes with a word that one of the gatekeepers says. If the child can't think of a rhyming word, he or she must kneel and pat the shoe of the gatekeeper to get through. Then the other gatekeeper gets a turn with the next child wanting to go through.

Gates of a City

Materials needed: small Legos® or other small building toys or blocks, small figures of people and animals

Directions: The children can build a round or square wall with "streets" and "houses" inside for the people and animals. Be sure the children leave at least one gateway in the wall for the people and animals to go through.

Active Play Center

The Fox and the Wall

Have the children form a line or circle to be the "wall." One child will be the "fox." Whenever the fox tries to break through the wall, those two nearest children should grab hands. See how soon the fox surprises the wall and gets through. This is a fun way for the children to see strength in working together.

Snack Time

Make a "wall" of sugar wafers or other square cookies. Since Nehemiah was the cupbearer to a king, use nice cups to serve fruit punch to the children, like sparkling clear plastic (disposable) ones. These come in several colors.

Prayer: Thank You, dear God, for helping the people work together to build a wall for You. Help me to work together with my friends, too. In Jesus' name, Amen.

Rebuilding the Wall

continued

"Working Together for God"

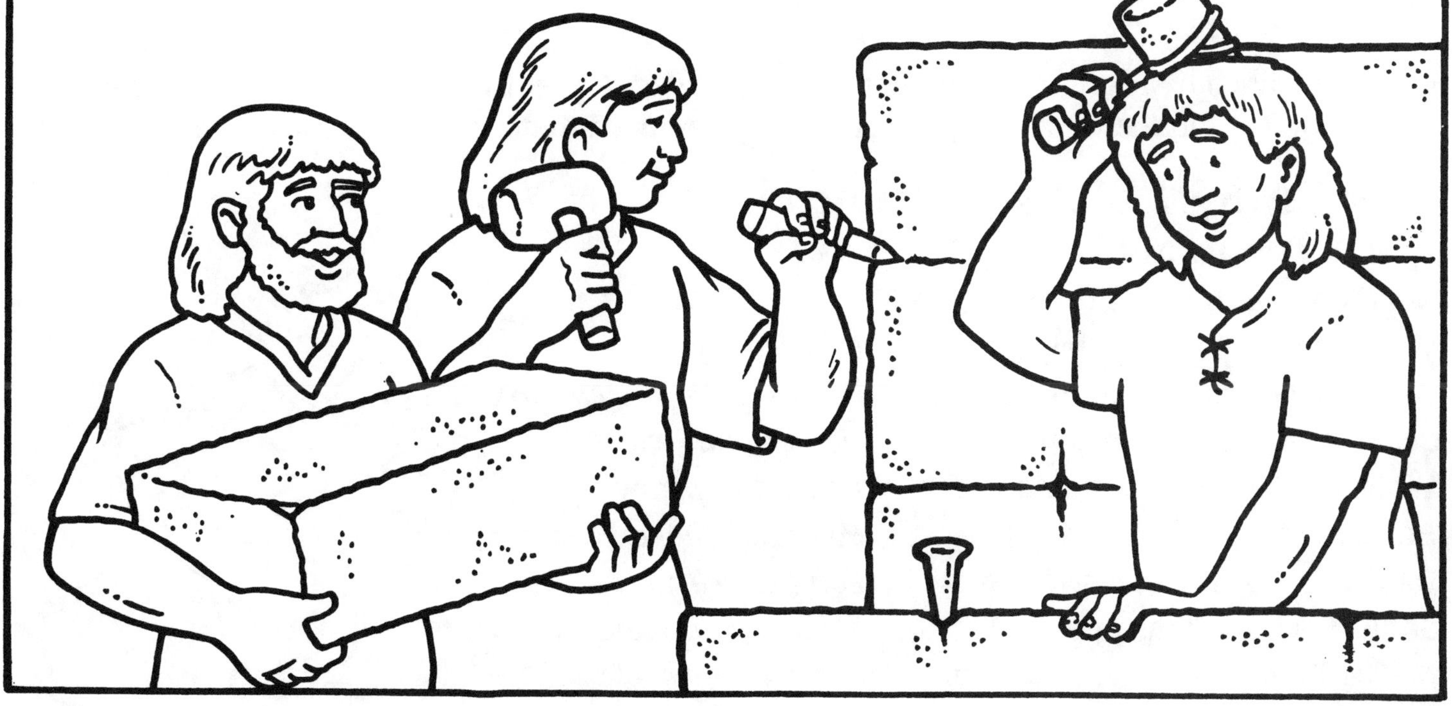

God Protects Daniel

(Based on Daniel 6)

Three times a day he got down on his knees and prayed . . . (Daniel 6:10)

Daniel was a very busy man—a top official in the empire of King Darius. But as busy as Daniel was, he still took time in his schedule to pray to God at least three times each and every day. Daniel's enemies were jealous of him, and they plotted to make it against the law to pray to God. But Daniel trusted God in good times and in bad. And God protected him abundantly—just as He will protect your kindergartners.

Nature, Blocks, and Playhouse Centers

Materials needed: realistic pictures and books about lions and about the story of Daniel; shaggy, gold-colored towels and small throw rugs; sashes

Directions: Discuss going to zoos with the children and seeing the lions there. See if the children can tell you some things about lions and some ways they differ from cats. (for example, size; danger—since they're wild; big mouths and teeth) Ask the children why we must be careful around lions. (so we don't get hurt) The children will enjoy making a large lion den or enclosure using blocks or boxes. Secure towels or rugs around the children using sashes to create lions. Pick someone to be Daniel and someone to be king and let the children act out the Bible story.

Active Play Center

Children will enjoy playing with lion or Daniel puzzles. Or, let them make a "lions' den" using small building blocks. They can put animal figures inside to act out this Bible story.

The Hungry Lions (Action Play)

Grrr! Grrr! Roar, roar!	(*Roar.*)
What do you think we're roaring for?	
We're hungry for some meat,	(*Rub tummy.*)
And Daniel's coming for us to eat.	(*Open mouth, pretend to bite.*)
See our big mouths open wide	(*Open mouth wide.*)
While they throw him right inside!	(*Pretend to throw.*)
But God says, "No; let Daniel be.	(*Point up; shake head; wag finger.*)
Daniel's a good man who loves Me."	(*Point to self.*)
So, instead, we lions purr—	(*Make purring noise.*)
Maybe Daniel will pet our soft fur.	(*Pretend to pet.*)

God Protects Daniel

continued

A Listening Lion

Materials needed: cuddly stuffed lion or other animal

Directions: Have the children sit in a circle. Tell them that prayer means talking to God. God wants us to talk to Him. We can pray every night when we go to bed. We can pray at mealtimes and thank God for our food. Hold up the lion and tell it something you'd like to praise or ask God about. Then pass this "listening lion" to the first child and have him or her do the same. You can offer suggestions, such as, "Can you tell the lion to tell God 'thank You' for your mother" or "new bike," etc. Pass the lion all around the circle. Then have the children talk to God to tell Him thank You for what they told the lion about.

Music Center

Daniel Prayed Three Times a Day

(Tune: "Merrily We Roll Along")

Daniel prayed three times a day, three times a day, three times a day.
Daniel prayed three times a day to love God and obe-ey.
"We don't like Daniel!" bad men said, bad men said, bad men said.
"We don't like Daniel!" bad men said. "Let's have him killed instea-ead."
They threw him in the lions' den, lions' den, lions' den.
They threw him in the lions' den and thought he'd be killed the-en.
But an angel God had sent, God had sent, God had sent.
But an angel God had sent, the lions to preve-ent.
"Are you all right?" the king did shout, king did shout, king did shout.
"Are you all right?" "Yes," Daniel said. And then he came right ou-ut!

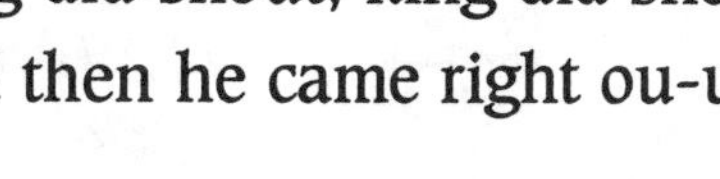

Art Center

A Good Time to Pray

Materials needed: one copy of page 57 per child, scissors, pencils, crayons, brad fasteners

Directions: After the children trace the numbers around the clock face, say the numbers with them. Discuss with them what the children in the pictures are doing. Have them color the pictures. Help the children cut out the clock hands and attach them with the brad fasteners. Tell the children that any time is a great time to talk to God.

God Protects Daniel

continued

Hungry Lion Puppets

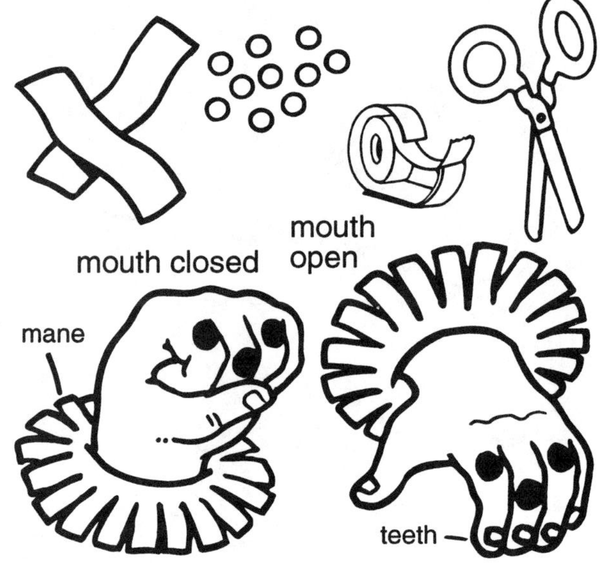

Materials needed: two 2" x 6" pieces of yellow paper per child (or pieces of yellow netting); scissors; tape or stapler; three 6 1/2" x 3/4" in diameter circles of black paper or adhesive covering per child, or use round adhesive labels and color them black (optional: 10 small white adhesive circles—about 1/4" diameter—per child)

Directions: Help the children make snips along one side of the yellow strips to make lion manes. Fit these around each child's wrist, making sure they are loose enough to slip on and off over their knuckles and tape or staple these strips together. Stick black circles on the fingers of each child's hand for eyes and a nose. (Optional: Stick the white circles on the children's fingernails for lions' teeth.) Let the children perform "The Hungry Lions" action play on page 54 or eat their snacks (see Snack Time below) at this time.

Games Center

Here Comes Daniel

Let each child take a turn being "Daniel" and slide down a slide. The others stand around the bottom of the slide pretending to be lions ready to pounce. Just before Daniel hits bottom, an "angel" says, "Freeze!" Then all the lions have to stop in those exact same poses without touching Daniel. Let the children see who has the funniest pose.

Race Around the Clock

Pick out certain parts of the room or playground to be the kitchen, the classroom, the church house, the park, and the bedroom. To help, you can mark the kitchen with a toy pot, the classroom with a book or toy chair, etc. Make sure the children know which room is which. Pretend to be the clock. Say, "Tick-tock, tick-tock, it is now 12 o'clock. Time to—eat!" Then the children race to kitchen. Or, say, "Nine o'clock—time for—school!", etc. Tell the children that no matter where we are or what we are doing, we can always talk to God.

Snack Time

Give each child a box of animal crackers with milk. Or, create a lion's face using a round cracker sandwich with raisins for eyes and shredded carrots for a mane.

God Protects Daniel

continued

Prayer

Today, instead of the regular prayer, you might ask the children to individually or all together tell God "thank You" for their food. Or say this:

Prayer: Thank You, dear God, for taking care of Daniel. I'm glad I can pray to You, too. In Jesus' name, Amen.

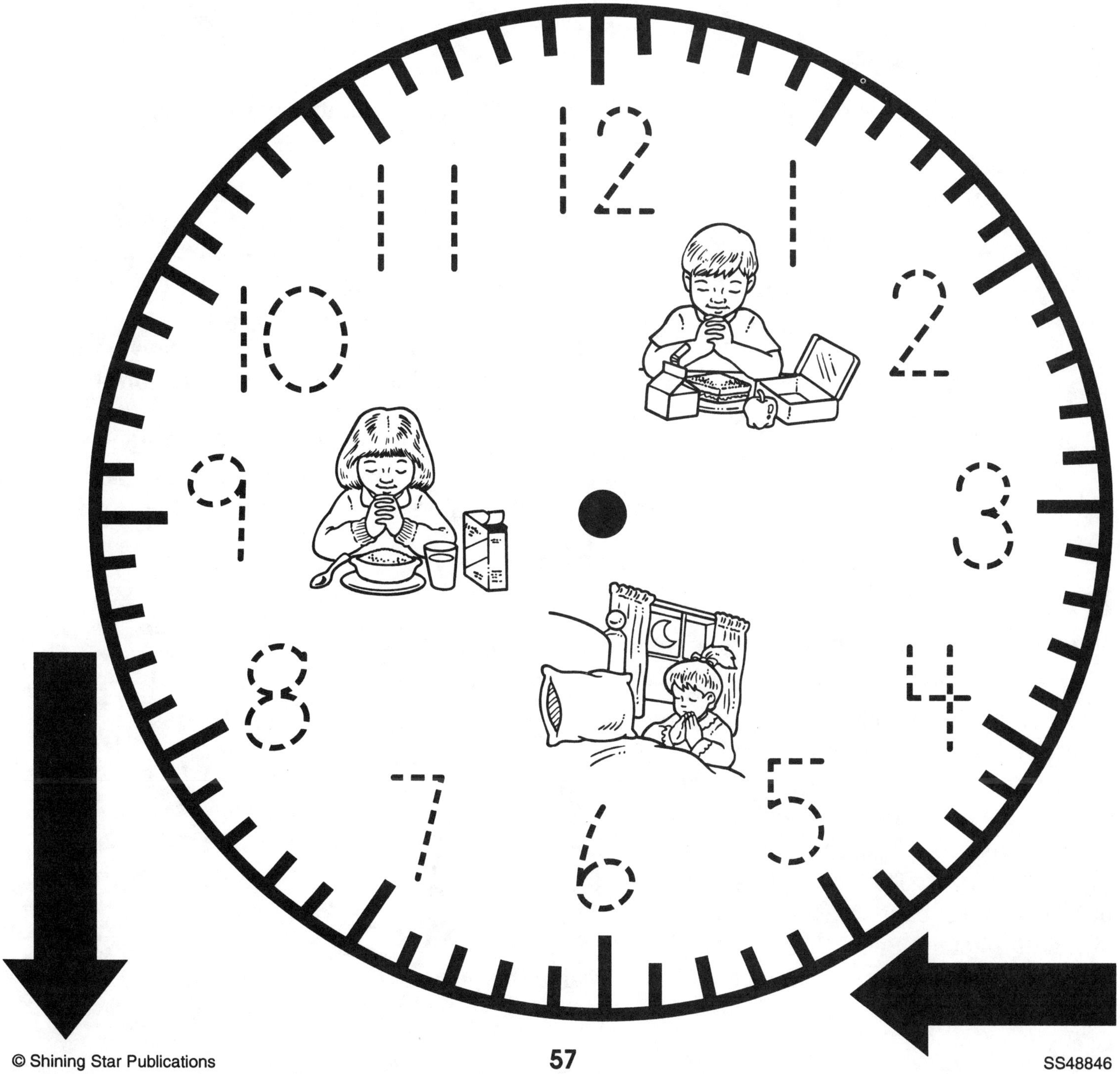

12 1 2 3 4 5 6 7 8 9 10 11

Jonah Is Sorry

(Based on Jonah 1–3)

From inside the fish Jonah prayed to the Lord . . . (Jonah 2:1)

God wanted Jonah to go to Nineveh and tell the people there to stop being bad. But Jonah did not want to go. So he packed his bags and started off in the opposite direction of Nineveh. Your kindergartners probably have a hard time obeying sometimes, too. Help them see that God wants them to be happy, and they will be happiest when they do the right thing.

Nature Center

A Storm at Sea

Materials needed: pictures and books about whales, giant squids, and giant fish; large pan or pool of water (put plastic under it if indoors); small plastic boats or bowls

Directions: Discuss large sea creatures with the children. Tell the children that animals can grow bigger in the water than on land because the water helps hold up their weight. Then let them place toy boats or bowls on the water surface very carefully. Tell them to notice how quiet the water is. Then have them blow on the water. Next, let the children put their hands in the water and stir it with all their might, seeing what happens when the small boats fill and sink to the bottom. Tell them that that's what a storm can do and that's why the sailors in this Bible story were so afraid.

Art Center

Jonah in a Whale

Materials needed: one copy of page 61, a lunch-size paper bag, and a rubber band per child; scissors; crayons; glue

Directions: Help the children put a rubber band around their lunch bags about 2" from the bottom. Turn the bag on its side. There is now a tail. Make sure the opening stays as large as possible; this is the whale's mouth. Have the children color and cut out their Jonah figures and eyes. They can glue the eyes on the outside of their bags. Then they can glue the two sides of Jonah together. Show them how to fold the flaps at the bottom so that Jonah can stand. They can glue the bottom of Jonah's stand inside the whale's tummy.

Jonah Is Sorry

continued

Music Center

Jonah's Journey

Because this song is long, you may wish to sing it by yourself, inviting the children to join in on the chorus.

(Tune: "Battle Hymn of the Republic")

"Jonah, go to Nineveh and preach God's Word for Me."
But Jonah said, "No, I won't go," and off he ran to sea.
He bought a ticket, climbed aboard, then sailed off speedily,
For he had disobeyed.

Chorus: Shame, oh, shame, oh, shame on Jonah!
Shame, oh, shame, oh, shame on Jonah!
Shame, oh, shame, oh, shame on Jonah!
For he had disobeyed.

That night while Jonah slept aboard the ship, a great wind blew.
"Help, help!" the sailors cried, afraid their ship would break in two.
"I'm sorry," Jonah said. "This storm is all my fault, it's true,
For I have disobeyed."

Chorus

"Please throw me in the water," Jonah said, "I did the sin."
And so they picked him up, and then, ker-splash! They threw him in.
Then just like that, the great wind stopped. The sea was calm again,
For he had disobeyed.

Chorus

A great fish swallowed Jonah up. Now he was quite afraid.
He thought of God's command to him and how he disobeyed.
"I'm sorry, I'll do better," was the promise Jonah made,
For he had disobeyed.

Chorus

God then told the fish to set him free again on land.
This time, Jonah listened and obeyed the Lord's command.
He went to Nineveh and preached God's Word on every hand.
Yes, Jonah now obeyed.

Chorus: I'm so glad, so glad for Jonah.
I'm so glad, so glad for Jonah.
I'm so glad, so glad for Jonah,
For Jonah now obeyed.

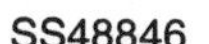

Jonah Is Sorry

continued

Games Center

Children will enjoy playing with various puzzles depicting Jonah or seas and boats. Let the children use Legos®, Tinkertoys®, or other small building toys to make boats.

Finding Jonah

Inside or outside, select a "Jonah" and a "whale." The whale closes his or her eyes while Jonah hides, and the other children help you count up to 20. Then the whale tries to find Jonah while everyone else yells "hot" or "cold." Give everyone who would like one a turn.

Active Play Center

The Happy Whale (Action Play)

Look at me! I'm a great big whale!	(*Hold arms out wide.*)
I'm big in my tummy and my head and my tail.	(*Point to tummy; point to head.*)
I swim through the water with a swish, swish, swish.	(*Move arms to swim.*)
All day long, I eat fish, fish, fish.	(*Smack lips.*)
God opened my mouth as wide as could be	(*Open mouth wide.*)
Then made Jonah fall right inside of me!	(*Gulp.*)
I took care of Jonah while I gave him a ride,	(*Pretend to swim.*)
And heard him praying to God inside.	(*Hand to ear, point to tummy.*)
I coughed Jonah right up on shore, and then	(*Pretend to cough.*)
I turned around and swam again.	(*Turn around; swim.*)

Playhouse and Blocks Centers

Some children may build a boat for Jonah, while others pretend to be residents of Nineveh, waiting for Jonah to visit them.

Snack Time

Give each child "fish crackers" on a "sea" of flavored gelatin or pudding, with fruit punch to drink.

Prayer: Thank You, dear God, for taking care of Jonah. Help me to obey You, too. In Jesus' name, Amen.

Jonah Is Sorry

continued

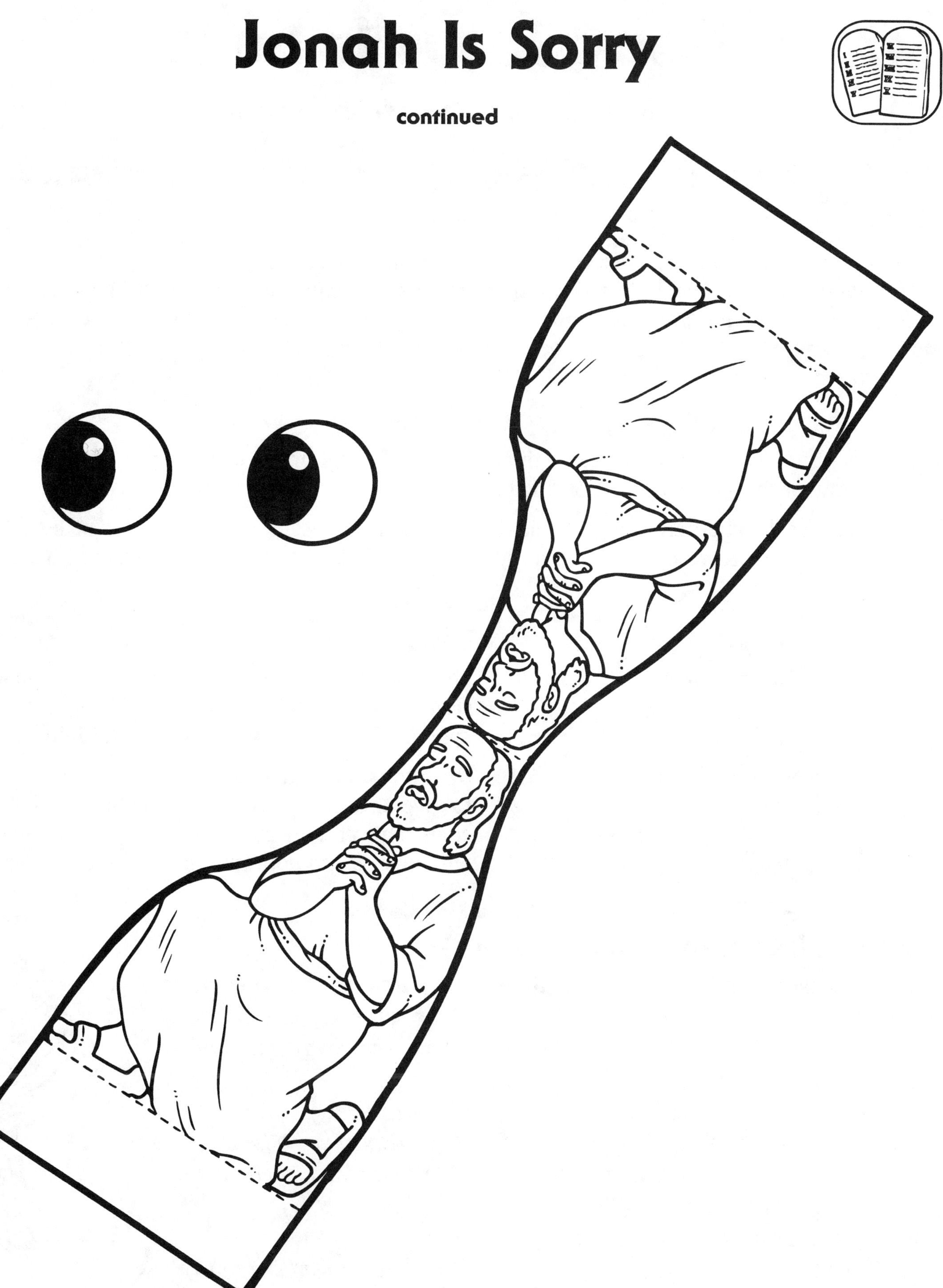

Baby Jesus Is Born

(Based on Matthew 2:1–12; Luke 2:1–20)

. . . Jesus was born in Bethlehem . . . (Matthew 2:1)

What a glorious time of year! There are enough riches of truth and joy in the Christmas story to fill several days or weeks. In a world that emphasizes Santa Claus and getting gifts, help the children see the greater joy and wonder of love and giving. Some of the activities in this chapter, such as the songs, can also be used as part of your Christmas program or presentation.

Nature Center

Materials needed: pictures and figures of camels, donkeys, horses, cattle, sheep; bale of hay, pile of straw or dry grass, or ears of dried corn; pictures of modest barns and stables

Directions: Let the children browse through the materials. Discuss the conditions of Jesus' birth (in a stable, animals present, etc.) with the children. Have them compare it to their births.

Games Center

Christmas Gifts

Materials needed: pile of familiar objects (nothing sharp), such as Bible storybook, block, doll, spoon, roll of tape, eraser, soft ball; blindfold

Directions: Let one child select one of the objects to give as a Christmas gift to the blindfolded child. This child tries to guess what it is. Give all who wish turns both as selectors and guessers.

Active Play Center

Three Wise Men (Action Play)

There once were wise men, one, two, three, *(Hold up one, two, then three fingers.)*
As wise, as wise, as wise could be. *(Look serious, point to head.)*
They rode on camels—plop, plop, plop, *(Move feet slowly like camels.)*
Beneath a star that did not stop. *(Point up.)*
Their camels all were carrying *(Point to back.)*
Treasures for a baby King. *(Point fingers up on head for crown.)*
Their way went up, then down a hill, *(Move hands up then down.)*
Till suddenly, that star stood still. *(Hold hands still.)*
Then all those gifts that they did bring *(Kneel.)*
They gave to Jesus, their new King. *(Put hands together to pray.)*

Baby Jesus Is Born

continued

Music Center

Keep joyful tapes of Christian, Christmastime music for the children to listen to quietly. Sing together old favorites like "Away in the Manger" with them. The songs below and on page 64 are easy to learn and lend themselves well to Christmas programs. This first song can also be recited without music. Also, children love singing the familiar song "Happy Birthday to You," addressing it to "dear Jesus."

Christmas Bells

(Tune: "Twinkle, Twinkle, Little Star")

Bells are ringing loud and clear
At this happy time of year,
Telling people, far and near,
Christmastime at last is here.
Bells are ringing loud and clear,
Bringing hope and joy and cheer!

Where, Oh, Where Was Our Lord Jesus Born?

(Tune: "Where, Oh, Where Has My Little Dog Gone?")

Where, oh, where was our Lord Jesus born?
Where, oh, where can it be?
In Bethlehem-town on the first Christmas morn,
I wish I'd been there to see!

Who, oh, who sang to shepherds that night?
Who, oh, who can it be?
A sky full of angels all glorious bright—
I wish I'd been there to see!

What, oh, what did the shepherds do then?
What, oh, what can it be?
They rushed to a stable in Bethlehem-town.
I wish I'd been there to see!

Why, oh, why were their hearts filled with joy?
Why, oh, why can it be?
Mary was holding a wee baby Boy.
I wish I'd been there to see!

Baby Jesus Is Born

continued

Sing a Song of Christmas!

Children will enjoy hitting triangles or ringing bells as they sing this song.

(Tune: "Sing a Song of Sixpence")

Sing a song of Christmas, a song of peace and joy;
In a lowly stable was born a baby Boy.
That baby Boy was Jesus, God's precious Son, we know.
So sing a song of Christmas because we love God so!

Art Center

Gifts to Show Love to Jesus

Materials needed: one or more copies of page 66 per child; colored gift tissue paper, cut in squares, diamonds, and triangles; circles cut from brightly-colored foil wrap; crayons; scissors; glue; tape; pieces of yarn or ribbon; Christmas potpourri or other small gifts

Directions: Let each child color a gift box pattern. Cut out and assemble the gift boxes. Let the children decorate the boxes with the materials listed above. Help the children place some colored tissue paper and some potpourri (or other small gift) inside their boxes. Add ribbon at one corner or create a handle so that each can hang from a tree.

Crowns for Kings

Materials needed: one copy of the crown pattern on page 67 on tagboard per child; small, brightly-colored foil shapes; crayons; scissors; glue; tape

Directions: Help the children color, cut out, and decorate their crowns with bits of foil shapes. Then help them fit the crowns to their heads. Despite the familiar song, "We Three Kings," the Bible doesn't say that the wise men were kings. However, we do know baby Jesus was a King because He is God's own Son. Let the children wear their crowns to act out this Bible story.

Baby Jesus Is Born

Christmas Cards to Share

Materials needed: one copy of the Holy Family, verse, and title patterns on page 67 per child; colored paper; crayons; scissors; glue (optional: glitter)

Directions: Help the children color and cut out their patterns. Then they can fold their sheets of colored paper twice in greeting card fashion. Show them how to glue the title on the cover, and their pictures and verses inside. The children may also draw sheep, a star, etc., around their pictures and add glitter if desired.

Nativity Scene

Materials needed: one enlarged copy of the Holy Family pattern on page 67 per child; colored paper; crayons; glue; straw, raffia, or dried peat moss

Directions: Have the children color and cut out the verse and picture and glue these onto colored paper. Next, they can add straw, raffia, or moss for a manger effect. (You could also back the pictures with cardboard and set them up as centerpieces for a creche scene, letting the children add plastic shepherd and animal figures.)

Playhouse and Blocks Centers

Children can build their own nativity scene, with places for the animals in the stable. Help the children dress up to act out the Bible story.

Snack Time

Give the children Christmas cookies or frosted cupcakes with a small container of red and green sprinkles they can sprinkle on themselves. Serve with fruit punch or milk.

Prayer: Thank You, dear God, for giving us baby Jesus, the best Christmas gift of all. In Jesus' name, Amen.

Baby Jesus Is Born

Fold back and glue.

Fold back and glue.

Fold back and glue.

Fold back and glue.

TOP

Fold back and glue.

Baby Jesus Is Born

continued

The Best Christmas Gift of All

. . . Jesus was born in Bethlehem . . .
(Matthew 2:1)

The Boy Jesus

(Based on Luke 2:41–52)

. . . they found him in the temple . . . (Luke 2:46)

What a privilege to be able to go to and feel at home in God's house! And what a comfort for the children to know that Jesus was once a child, too, and can understand the problems children face.

Playhouse Center and Nature Walk

Walking to Jerusalem

After dressing up with items from the dress-up chest, have the children walk outside or inside around the church, pretending to be walking with the boy Jesus and His family from their home to the temple. Encourage the children to tell you discoveries, such as ants or clouds, that Jesus might have seen and enjoyed on His journey, too. They might also enjoy singing a song (such as the first one below) as they walk, just as God's people did long ago.

Music Center

Children might enjoy listening to tapes of choir or organ music. They will also enjoy using rhythm instruments or clapping along to the songs below and on page 69. Discuss the words of the songs with the children.

Jesus Was a Little Child Once

After singing the words below, the children may also wish to sing the original lyrics to this song.

(Tune: "Jesus Loves the Little Children")

Jesus was a little child once,
A little child like you and me.
Jesus did His chores and played
And a lot of friends He made.
Jesus loved and helped God and His family.

I would like to be like Jesus,
Growing wise and growing strong,
Showing love to everyone
Just like Jesus, God's dear Son,
Doing what is right and never what is wrong!

The Boy Jesus

continued

This Is the Way We Go to Church

(Tune: "This Is the Way We Wash Our Clothes")

This is the way we go to church,
Go to church, go to church.
This is the way we go to church
Early Sunday morning.

This is the way we sing to God,
Sing to God, sing to God.
This is the way we sing to God
Early Sunday morning.

This is the way we hear God's Word . . .

This is the way we pray to God . . .

12 Birthday Candles

This song is fun to sing to celebrate Jesus' twelfth birthday. Have the children form a circle. Pass a large candle from child to child as you all sing this song.

(Tune: "Ten Little Indians")

One little, two little, three little candles,
Four little, five little, six little candles,
Seven little, eight little, nine little candles,
Ten, and eleven, and twelve.

The child who is holding the candle when you say the word "twelve" then gets in the middle of the circle, holding the candle, while everyone pretends to blow it out.

Active Play Center

When Jesus Was Little (Action Play)

Jesus was once a baby small. (*Measure small with hands.*)
He couldn't walk or talk at all. (*Shake head.*)
He'd suck His thumb and pat His hand. (*Pretend to suck; pat.*)
He learned to crawl and then to stand. (*Crawl; stand up.*)
One year old, then two, then three, (*Hold up 1, 2, then 3 fingers.*)
Then four, then five years old like me. (*Hold up 4 fingers, then 5.*)
Jesus knows how I should be (*Point up, then to self.*)
'Cause He was once a child like me. (*Point up, then to self.*)

The Boy Jesus

continued

Art Center

A Roll of Scroll

Materials needed: one copy of page 71 per child, pencils, crayons, ribbon, Bible storybook, a scroll (you can make)

Directions: Help the children complete the maze of Jesus' trip to the temple. Then have them help Mary and Joseph find their way and color their mazes. Tell the children that when Jesus went to God's house, the Bibles He saw didn't look like ours. Show them the Bible storybook. Tell the children that long ago, the information from the Bible was written on scrolls that looked like the one you have. Show them the scroll. Help the children roll up their finished pictures either in one roll or in two rolls that meet in the center to create scrolls. Tie with a ribbon.

Games Center

Hurrying to Jerusalem

Divide the children into two teams. Designate a tree or other object to be Jerusalem. Give a scroll to the first child on each team. Each child runs to Jerusalem, tags the object that represents Jerusalem, and then returns and gives the scroll to you. You then hand it to the next person on that team. See which teams finishes first.

Where Is Jesus?

This is basically a hide-and-seek game, with one child pretending to be the boy Jesus and the others looking for Him.

Blocks Center

Children can build a temple or a church they can use to act out this Bible story. Be sure the children make room for seats for Jesus and His teachers. Include a Bible storybook.

Snack Time

When God's people went to the temple, they usually feasted for joy. Your children can have a joyful birthday party for Jesus any time of year with cupcakes, milk, and a scoop of ice cream.

Prayer: Thank You, dear God, for helping Jesus do the right thing, and for helping me do the right thing, too. In Jesus' name, Amen.

The Boy Jesus

continued

Jesus Calls His Disciples

(Based on Matthew 4:18–22)

"Come, follow me," Jesus said . . . (Matthew 4:19)

Jesus' followers loved Him. They listened to Him. They enjoyed talking to Him. And then many of them went right back to doing what they had been doing before. Jesus helped some of His followers see that He was calling them for more than that. He wanted them to stay with Him always and teach others about God.

Nature Center

Materials needed: aquarium or goldfish in bowl, pictures of fish (optional: fishnet)

Directions: Help the children discuss the special abilities God has given fish—they can breathe under water, and they can swim with fins and tails. Show the children how the fish can't get through the net.

Games Center

Let's Go Fishing!

Materials needed: butterfly, fishing, or other small net; wadded up balls of paper to be "flying fish"

Directions: Have one child throw a fish in the air toward the child with the net. The child with the net tries to catch the fish.

Blocks Center

Building a Boat

Children can build a boat to go fishing in just as Peter, Andrew, James, and John did. Be sure they include seats and a sail or oars (but don't let them hit anyone with the oars).

Art Center

A Boat Race

Help the children make boats the old-fashioned way that can also be used to make hats or drinking cups. To make a boat, fold a sheet of paper in half crosswise. Then fold down two equal flaps on one side; fold up the remaining paper at the bottom on both sides. Let the children decorate their boats. Place them in a line on the floor or a table. Have the children blow on them to race them.

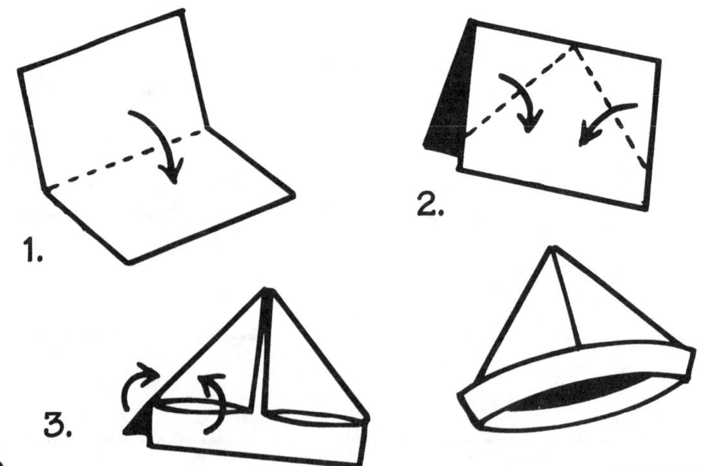

Jesus Calls His Disciples

continued

Playhouse Center

Telling About Jesus

Let the children play with phones, pretending to tell others about Jesus. Or, let them use the dress-up chest and tea party dishes to invite neighbors over whom they can tell about Jesus.

Active Play Center

Let's Be Fish!

Let the children ride around the playground in a parade of tricycles, wagons, etc. They can pretend they are disciples going around telling others about Jesus. Or, let them play a game in which they recite the verse below with you. One child is Peter, and Peter has a small piece of net or a net bag (such as the kind produce comes in). The rest of the children are fish, and they stand and move their arms as if they are swimming. When the children hear the word "yet" in the verse, they run, and Peter tries to touch one with his net. That touched child then becomes Peter.

Swish, swish! I'm a fish!
To swim all day's my only wish.
Here comes Peter with his net.
But Peter hasn't caught me YET!

Peter and Andrew and James and John (Action Play)

Peter and Andrew and James and John	(*Hold up 1, 2, 3, and then 4 fingers.*)
Had fished and fished all night.	(*Yawn; rub eyes.*)
But no matter how hard they tried,	(*Shake head.*)
Those fish just would not bite.	(*Bite.*)
Jesus came down to the lake to see.	(*Move hands like ripples.*)
He saw the sad, tired men.	(*Put hand above eyes.*)
He said, "Peter and Andrew and James and John,	(*Hold up 1, 2, 3, and then 4 fingers.*)
Why don't you go fishing again?"	
Peter and Andrew and James and John	(*Hold up 1, 2, 3, and then 4 fingers.*)
All said, "It's no use, we think."	(*Look sad; throw up hands.*)
But they tried again—and their nets were so full,	(*Spread arms wide apart to measure.*)
Their poor boats started to sink!	(*Move arms toward floor.*)
Peter and Andrew and James and John	(*Hold up 1, 2, 3, and then 4 fingers.*)
Said, "You are God's Son, we see."	(*Point up.*)
"Put your fishing away," Jesus said.	(*Smile.*)
"I want you to follow Me."	(*Point out, then to self.*)

Jesus Calls His Disciples

continued

Helping Peter Fish

Materials needed: one copy of page 75 per child, pencils, crayons (optional: scissors; dry elbow macaroni, fish crackers, cotton balls; glue; heavy paper; fine netting, such as is used for produce or clothing)

Directions: Help the children complete their dot-to-dot pictures and color them. Their pictures can be used as is, or have them cut them out on the heavy line and glue them onto heavy paper. The children could also glue on macaroni waves, cracker fish, cotton clouds, or a fishnet.

Music Center

Children may listen to ocean sounds tapes. Or, let them sing the song below.

Out in the Deep Blue Sea

(Tune: "Oh, How I Love Jesus")

Peter went to go fishing,
Peter went to go fishing,
Peter went to go fishing,
Out in the deep blue sea.

He fished all night but caught nothing,
He fished all night but caught nothing,
He fished all night but caught nothing,
Out in the deep blue sea.

Jesus said, "Try again now,"
Jesus said, "Try again now,"
Jesus said, "Try again now,"
Out in the deep blue sea.

Peter did what He told him,
Peter did what He told him,
Peter did what He told him,
Out in the deep blue sea.

His nets were now crammed full of fishes,
His nets were now crammed full of fishes,
His nets were now crammed full of fishes,
Out in the deep blue sea.

Snack Time

Serve fish crackers and pretzel sticks in a net bag with lemonade.

Prayer: Thank You, dear God, for helping Peter and Andrew and James and John, and for helping me, too. In Jesus' name, Amen.

Jesus Calls His Disciples

continued

Peter and Andrew obeyed Jesus.

Jesus Feeds 5000

(Based on Mark 6:30–44)

Give thanks to the God of heaven . . . (Psalm 136:26)

Children love hearing about the little boy who shared his lunch—and about Jesus' wonderful ability to feed everyone. How exciting to know that Jesus loves us so much, He doesn't even want us to go hungry! Emphasize the joy of eating and the need to always thank God for our food before eating, just as Jesus did.

Sand Center

The children can make a "road" in the sand with their fingers. Encourage the children to set up twig trees and pebble rocks by the road. Then the children can walk plastic figurines or their fingers along the road to go hear Jesus talk.

Music Center

Thank You, God

Let the children listen to songs about Jesus on cassettes. Or, they can sing the song below, clapping along in time to the music.

(Tune: "Three Blind Mice")

Thank You, God, thank You, God,
For my food, for my food.
For all the good things I like to eat,
For bread and vegetables, fruit, and meat,
And chocolate chip cookies that taste so sweet,
Thank You, God, thank You, God.

Playhouse Center, Nature Walk, and Story Time

Going to Hear Jesus

At a play stove, let the children pretend to cook a lunch to take with them to hear Jesus.

Let the children dress up in old clothes or in towels secured with cloth sashes. They can walk or parade around outside in good weather or around the room. Encourage the children to imagine what birds, trees, etc., the little boy would have seen on his way to hear Jesus. End up at the story rug and tell this Bible story there.

Jesus Feeds 5000

continued

Pictures Center

Jesus Loves the Little Children

Materials needed: magazines; catalogs; scissors; a picture of Jesus teaching or one of Jesus with children around Him, or one of Jesus alone

Directions: Put up a picture of Jesus. Let the children cut out pictures of children from the magazines or catalogs to place around Jesus' picture.

Thankful for Food Mural

Materials needed: large piece of newsprint (or the back of a long piece of wallpaper), markers, pictures of food from newspapers and magazines, glue, scissors

Directions: Print "Thank You, God, for our food" on the piece of newsprint. Let the children cut out the pictures, glue them around the mural, and then sign their names.

Active Play Center

To Hear Jesus (Action Play)

"Here's your lunch," his mother said,	(*Pretend to hand lunch bag over.*)
"To eat when you hear Jesus."	(*Put hand to mouth, and then to ear.*)
So down the road, the little boy skipped	(*Skip in place.*)
To the place where he'd hear Jesus.	(*Put hand to ear.*)
5000 people were sitting there,	(*Sit.*)
All wanting to hear Jesus.	(*Put hand to ear.*)
Jesus talked until time for lunch.	(*Put hand to tummy.*)
How the people loved to hear Jesus!	(*Clap; put hand to ear.*)
"Feed them," Jesus told His friends.	(*Point out.*)
The little boy could hear Jesus.	(*Put hand to ear.*)
"Share my lunch," the little boy said,	(*Pretend to hold up bag.*)
"With everyone who hears Jesus."	(*Spread arms wide; put hand to ear.*)
Five loaves of bread and two little fish	(*Hold up five fingers on one hand and two on the other.*)
Fed everyone who heard Jesus.	(*Put hand to ear.*)
I'm so glad for that little boy,	(*Clap.*)
And I'm glad that I can hear Jesus!	(*Clap; put hand to ear; point up.*)

Jesus Feeds 5000

continued

Let's Catch Fish for Lunch

Materials needed: five small plastic bags (or toe ends of large, light-colored socks); rubber bands; beans, plastic pellets, or wadded-up small paper pieces (children will enjoy helping with that!); wastebasket

Directions: Fill the bags with beans, pellets, or paper wads. Secure each with a large rubber band, leaving some plastic sticking out for a tail. Draw eyes and smiles on your fish. Encourage the children to toss the fish into a wastebasket fishing pail about five feet away.

Blocks and Small Games Centers

Ask the children where the people will sit to listen to Jesus. Tell the children to build seats—large or small—using blocks or Legos® for themselves or for toy figures to sit on.

Art Center

Thankful Place Mats

Materials needed: one copy of page 79 per child, crayons

Directions: Have the children connect the dots to depict the loaves and fishes. Read the thank-you prayer to the children and help them learn it. After the children have colored their place mats, let them use them for snack time, or they can take them home to show their parents.

Making Lunch for a Little Boy

Materials needed: play dough or clay, disposable plates

Directions: The children will enjoy making loaves and fishes for the little boy's lunch—or they could make other food they think he might like.

Snack Time

The children will enjoy making their own lunch snacks of crackers and peanut butter or cheese spread. Or, they may spread smooth tuna salad on bread slices. Help them cut their sandwiches in half with a dull knife.

Prayer: Recite together the prayer on the place mats the children make.

Jesus Feeds 5000

continued

Thank You, God, for My Food

Thank You, God, for food to eat.
Thank You, God, for friends we meet.
Thank You, God, for my family.
Thank You, God, for loving me.

In Jesus' name, Amen.

Jesus Saves a Little Girl

(Based on Luke 8:40–42, 49–56)

. . . he took her by the hand and said, "My child, get up!" (Luke 8:54)

Jesus was very important and popular. People gathered around Him everywhere He went. But He was never too busy to help children and their parents while He was here on earth. And be sure the children know that He's still never too busy to help them today!

Music Center

Children will enjoy singing favorites like "Jesus Loves Me" and "Jesus Loves the Little Children," as well as the song below. Also, you could let the children tape a song or a message for a sick friend.

Jairus' Daughter

(Tune: "London Bridge")

Jesus, Jesus, please come quick,
Please come quick, please come quick.
Somebody is very sick—
It's Jairus' daughter.

Then Jesus came, but people said,
People said, people said,
"You're too late; somebody's dead—
It's Jairus' daughter."

But Jesus told the girl to rise,
Girl to rise, girl to rise.
Who came alive, to their surprise?
It's Jairus' daughter!

Nature Center

Materials needed: small adhesive bandages, tongue depressors, mirror, toy phone (optional: stethoscope)

Directions: Under supervision, let the children discuss what certain medications are for, when they should be used, and who should apply them. Be sure to emphasize that they should never, never open a medicine container by themselves and take some. Encourage the children to know their full name, address, and phone number, as well as how to dial 911 in an emergency. Tell them that when someone is sick, we should pray for him or her. Let the children use the materials to pretend one of them is sick or hurt. One child can put on a bandage, one can call 911, etc. Let them role-play a variety of situations.

Jesus Saves a Little Girl

continued

Active Play Center

The children can play paramedics or ambulance drivers as they ride around the playground taking sick toy animals to the hospital. On the slide, they can pretend they're going up the hospital elevator as they climb, and then slide down when they're all well again. The children will enjoy using small building toys to build a road so that they can drive a sick person to the doctor's office or hospital.

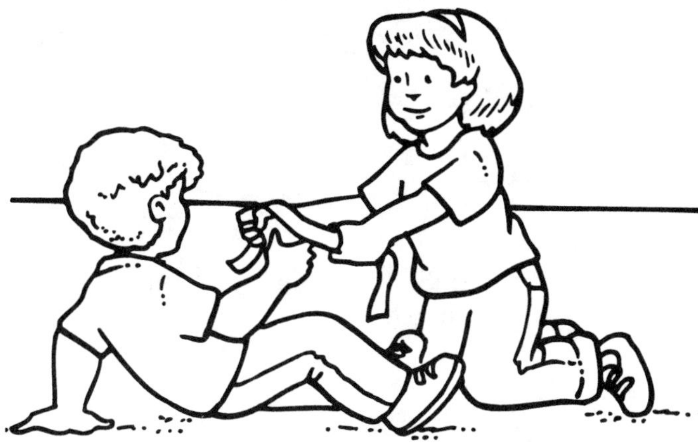

We All Fall Down

Have the children form a circle, hold hands, and sing the song below. When they hear the word "down," they all fall. Then they can pretend to be doctors, helping each other after the fall.

(Tune: "Ring Around the Rosy")

Ring around the rosy,
Don't fall on your nose-y.
Uh-oh, uh-oh—don't fall DOWN!

A Sick Little Girl (Action Play)

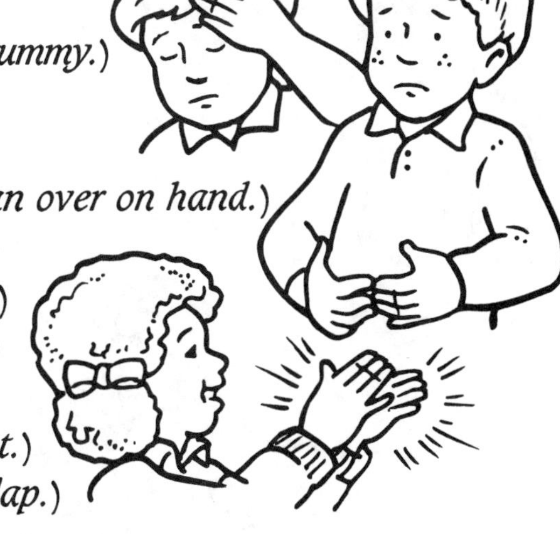

I'm sick. My tummy hurts a lot. (*Look sad; hold tummy.*)
My head feels strange and very hot. (*Hold head.*)
Don't want to run and play. Instead, (*Shake head.*)
I only want to go to bed. (*Lie down or lean over on hand.*)
Mom tells Dad, "Our poor girl's sick. (*Pretend to cry.*)
Go tell Jesus—tell Him quick!" (*Pretend to run.*)
Everybody's crying now. (*Pretend to cry.*)
They want me well, but don't know how. (*Shake head.*)
But Jesus takes my hand, and then, (*Reach hand out.*)
Just like that, I'm well again! (*Jump up and clap.*)

Art Center

Healing a Sick Girl

Materials needed: one copy of the pattern on page 82 per child, crayons, scissors, tape, one sheet of paper per child

Directions: After children color and cut out their figure of the girl, show them how to fold their sheet of paper in half, tape closed the long side and one short side to make the girl's bed or sleeping bag. Then the children can act out the Bible story, sliding the girl's figure into the bed when she's sick and pulling her out when she's well again.

Jesus Saves a Little Girl

continued

Playhouse and Blocks Centers

When We're Sick

Children can build a house for Jairus and his family and then dress up and act out this Bible story. Or, they can play doctor and nurse and make a doctor's office or hospital. Other children, dolls, or stuffed animals can be patients. Ask the children who we can always talk to when we're sick and scared—even if Mommy and Daddy aren't there. Tell them the answer is Jesus. He loves us and wants to help us get better quick.

Snack Time

When Jesus healed the sick girl, He told her family to feed her. The children can pretend to be Jairus' daughter as they eat miniature marshmallows and fresh fruit.

Prayer: Thank You, dear God, for being with me when I'm sick and helping me to get all better. In Jesus' name, Amen.

Two Sisters and Jesus

(Based on Luke 10:38–42)

. . . Martha opened her home to him. (Luke 10:38)

What if we could invite Jesus into our own home? That is the joy and wonder of this Bible story, for, of course, we can. Help the children think how they can help make their own homes where Jesus is always welcome.

Music Center

The children will enjoy singing favorites like "Jesus Loves Me" and "Jesus Loves the Little Children," as well as the song below.

I Love Jesus

(Tune: "Twinkle, Twinkle, Little Star")

I love Jesus, yes, I do,
And I know He loves me, too.
Jesus helps me sing and play
And to have a happy day.
I love Jesus, yes, I do,
And I know He loves me, too.

To Show Our Love to Jesus

(Tune: "Lazy Mary, Won't You Get Up?")

"Mary, Mary, won't you come here,
Won't you come here, won't you come here?
The house won't be finished in time, I fear,
To show our love to Jesus."
So Mary helped clean the house up neat,
The house up neat, the house up neat,
Then sat and listened at Jesus' feet
To show her love to Jesus.
"Jesus, Jesus," then Martha said,
Martha said, Martha said,
"My sister should help me to cook instead,
To show her love to Jesus."
"Martha, Martha, how good you are,
How good you are, how good you are,
But listening to Jesus is better far,
To show your love to Jesus."

Two Sisters and Jesus

continued

Nature Center

Materials needed: bottle of dish detergent, pan or sink of water, sponges, paper towels

Directions: Ask the children why Mary and Martha needed to clean things up. Ask them why we need to wash our hands before we eat. Discuss with them how soap and water help clean away dirt and germs. Let the children help sponge off tables and countertops.

Active Play Center

Let the children build a road so that Jesus can go to Mary and Martha's house. They will also enjoy acting out the song on page 83, "To Show Our Love to Jesus."

On a warm day outside, let the children play toss with wet sponges (if properly dressed), or they can pretend they are going to the store for groceries and bringing them home. Ask the children what they would like to have for Jesus to eat, if He were to come to their house.

Shopping for Cheese and Potatoes

Materials needed: plastic sponges, beanbags, large plastic bucket or bushel basket

Directions: Tell the children to pretend that the bucket or basket is the shopping basket, the sponges are cheese, and the beanbags are potatoes. Have the children stand six or seven feet back from the basket and see if they can throw all their groceries in it.

A Mouse in Martha's House (Action Play)

I'm a mouse in Martha's house. (*Smile.*)
I have to run and hide. (*Curl up in ball.*)
Each time I speak, I make a squeak. (*Make squeaking sound.*)
She wants no mice inside. (*Frown; shake head.*)
She sweeps her broom in every room (*Pretend to sweep.*)
And makes her windows shine. (*Pretend to wash windows.*)
"For Jesus dear," she says, "things here (*Point up.*)
Should all look clean and fine." (*Nod head.*)
Uh-oh! There's more crumbs on the floor (*Point.*)
That Martha hasn't seen. (*Peer.*)
I help them roll into my hole. (*Pretend to roll crumbs.*)
Now everything is clean! (*Clap hands.*)

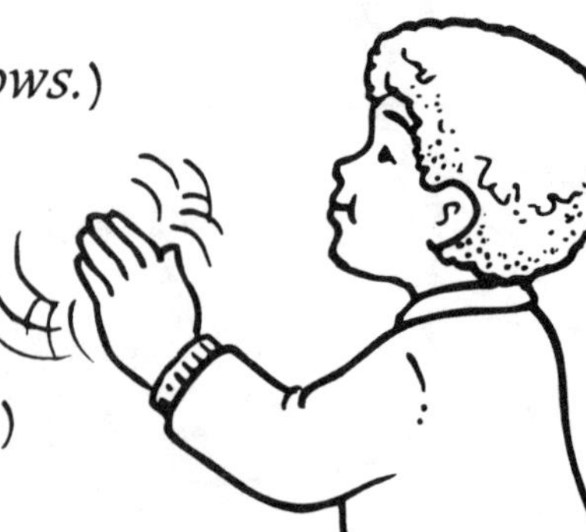

Two Sisters and Jesus

continued

Playhouse and Blocks Centers

Jesus Is Coming!

Let the children use playhouse fixtures and blocks to build a house to act out this Bible story. They can also use toy or pretend pots, pans, brooms, dishes, etc., to get their house ready. You could also let them dress up.

Art Center

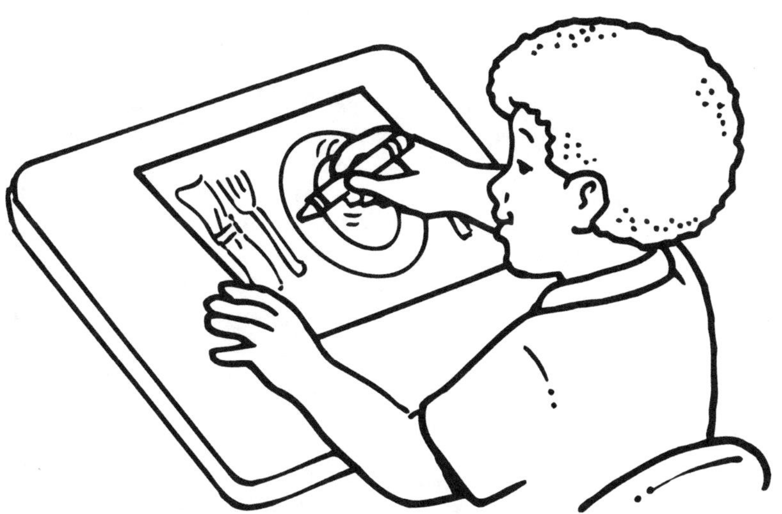

Preparing a Meal for Jesus

Materials needed: one copy of page 86 per child, crayons (optional: glue, paper napkins, stickers)

Directions: Encourage the children to draw on the plates what they think Jesus would like to eat. Have them color their pictures. They can also add stickers to their plates, and glue a real napkin beside the fork.

Snack Time

As you serve peanut butter and jelly sandwiches with milk, remind the children that Jesus is right there with them. You can serve the sandwiches on paper plates you put on top of the ones they colored.

Prayer: Thank You, dear God, for being right here with us and for loving us. In Jesus' name, Amen.

Two Sisters and Jesus

continued

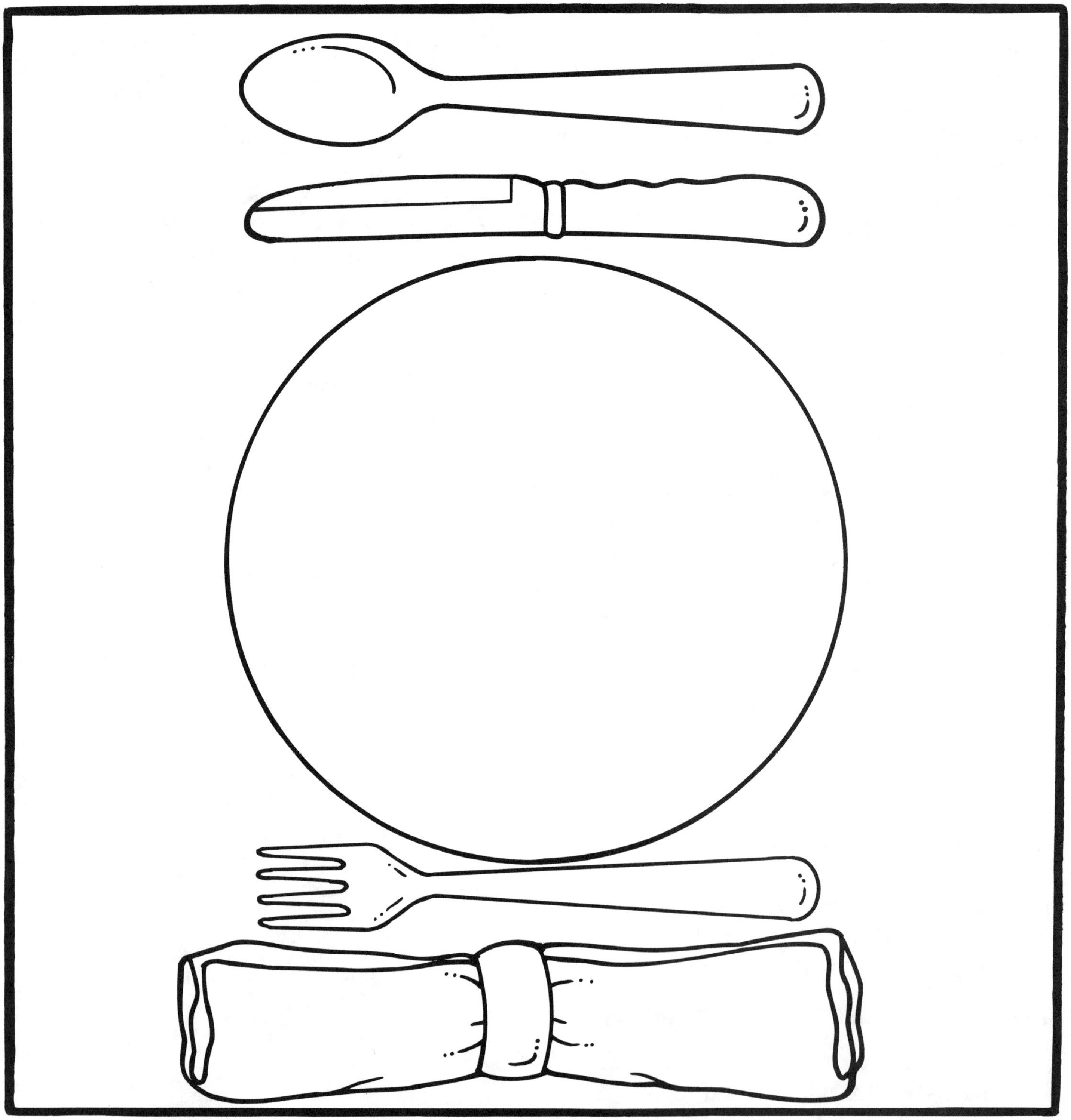

Jesus Calls the Children

(Based on Mark 10:13–16)

. . . *"Let the little children come to me . . . "* (Mark 10:14)

Jesus' disciples thought their Lord was much too busy and important to bother with little children. But Jesus never thought so! In fact, He told His followers that little children had the purest and most loving hearts of all. And then He picked up and hugged every one of those little ones!

Music Center

Have the children listen to tapes of bird calls (such as children walking to hear Jesus might have heard), or tapes of favorite Christian children's songs. They could sing "Jesus Loves Me," "Jesus Loves the Little Children," or "I Love Jesus" from page 83. Or, let them sing the song below.

Mother, May I?

(Tune: "Are You Sleeping?")

"Mother, may I go see Jesus?"
"Yes, my dear; yes, my dear.
He'll be glad to see you, He'll be glad to see you.
Never fear, never fear."

"Mother, may I say I love Him?"
"Yes, my dear; yes, my dear.
He will hug and bless you, He will hug and bless you.
Never fear, never fear."

"Mother, may I hug Him back then?"
"Yes, my dear; yes, my dear.
He will love you always, He will love you always.
Never fear, never fear."

Nature Walk With Story Time

Let's Go Hear Jesus!

Let the children walk around the playground or church grounds, pretending they are going to hear Jesus preach. Encourage them to note the grass, trees, butterflies, and other beauty around them. (In poor weather, they can walk around inside the church or school building.) At the story rug inside or a nice spot outside, have the children sit as you tell this Bible story. Afterward, give each child a hug and say, "God, please bless (child's name). In Jesus' name, Amen." Then encourage them to share Jesus' love for them by hugging each other.

Jesus Calls the Children

continued

Active Play Center

When Jesus Tells the Children, "Come"

Outside or inside, wherever you have lots of room, point out to the children a spot called "home" and a spot called "where Jesus sat." Then when you teach the children the song below (tune: "London Bridge"), tell the children to race from "home" to "where Jesus sat" when they hear the word "run" the first time. When they hear "run" the second time, they go back "home."

When Jesus tells the children, "Come," children, "Come,"
children, "Come,"
When Jesus tells the children, "Come," everybody RUN!
When Mother says, "Come back home now, back home now, back home now,"
When Mother says, "Come back home now," everybody RUN!

Under the Spreading Green Tree (Action Play)

Jesus was sitting and teaching the people	*(Sit.)*
Under the spreading green tree.	*(Reach arms up and out like a tree.)*
He told the fathers and mothers, "I love you.	*(Put hand on heart.)*
I'll help you. Please come unto Me."	*(Point out, then to self.)*
Children were sitting there listening also	*(Put hand to ear.)*
Under the spreading green tree.	*(Reach arms up and out like a tree.)*
The children jumped up and ran to see Jesus	*(Jump up; pretend to run.)*
When He said, "Please come unto Me."	*(Point out, then to self.)*
"No, no, children! No!" cried Jesus' disciples	*(Shake head and finger.)*
Under the spreading green tree.	*(Reach arms up and out like a tree.)*
"Don't bother Jesus. He's talking to grown-ups	*(Frown; shake head.)*
When He says, 'Please come unto Me.'"	*(Point out, then to self.)*
But Jesus said, "I'm also talking to children	*(Smile; open arms.)*
Under the spreading green tree.	*(Reach arms up and out like a tree.)*
I want you to know that I always will love you.	*(Open arms wide.)*
So, children, please come unto Me."	*(Point out, then to self.)*

Playhouse and Blocks Centers

Let's Go See Jesus!

Children will enjoy dressing up the whole family (including dolls and stuffed animals) to get ready to go see Jesus. They can also use blocks to build a road for the happy trip.

Jesus Calls the Children

continued

Games Center

Pass It On

Materials needed: heart or empty heart-shaped candy box (this object will symbolize a loving heart)

Directions: Have the children sit in a circle. The first child whispers, "Jesus loves you. Pass it on," and hands the loving heart to the next child. Repeat this around the circle. When the children are familiar with this game, divide them into two teams in lines or circles and see which can pass both a message and the loving heart to the end first.

Art Center

Someone Jesus Loves

Materials needed: one copy of boy or girl pattern on page 90 per child, crayons, scissors, glue (optional: stapler, Cheerios® or other dry O-shaped cereal, or dried raffia or peat moss for "hair"; craft sticks, sturdy pieces of cardboard, or 1" x 6" pieces of wood for handles)

Directions: Tell the children to color their patterns and cut them out. Next, they should fold at the top of the head, and glue the two sides together. (Optional: They could add raffia or moss "hair" or cereal "curls." You could also staple on a handle and write each child's name on the handle.)

Snack Time

Sprinkle Cheerios® or other dry O-shaped cereal or heart-shaped candies on pudding or flavored gelatin. Serve with fruit drink.

Prayer: Thank You, dear God, for loving us always. In Jesus' name, Amen.

Jesus Calls the Children

continued

Someone
Jesus
Loves

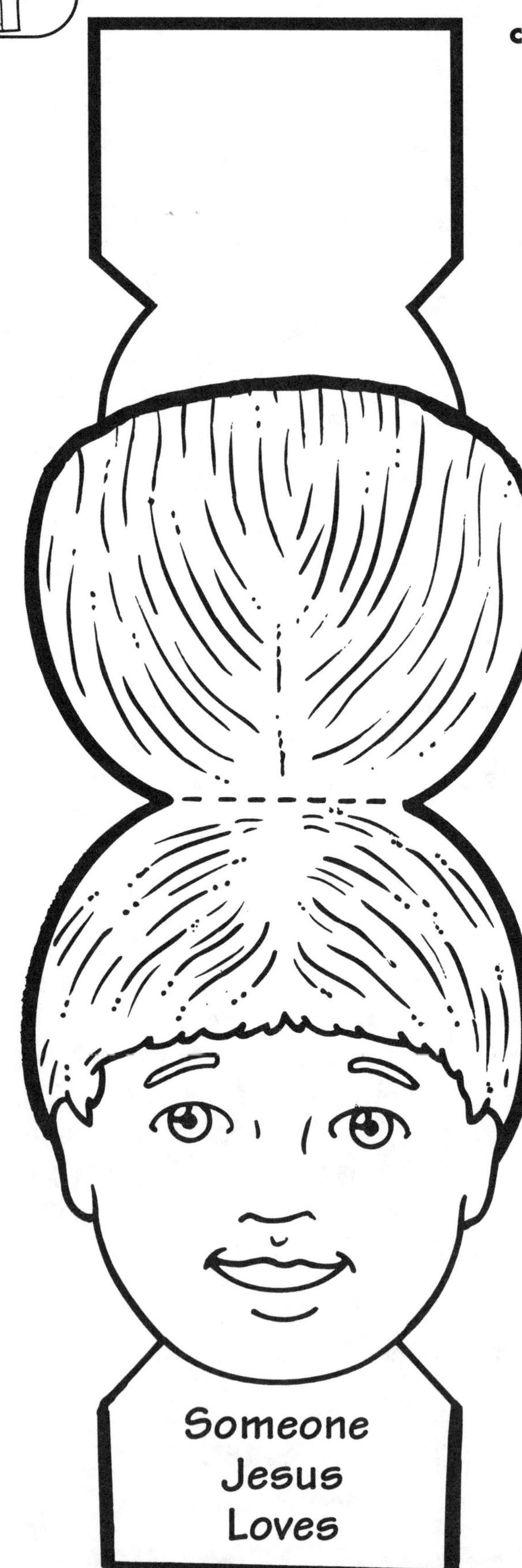

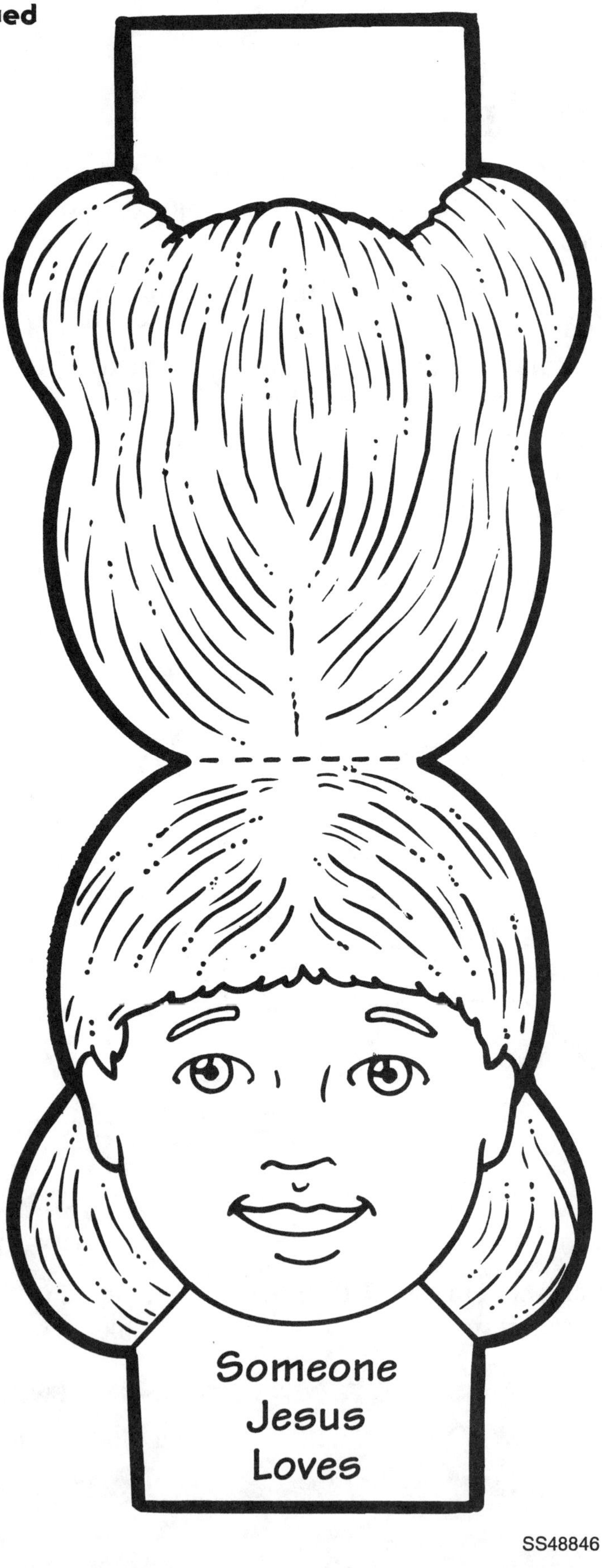
Someone
Jesus
Loves

Jesus Calls Zacchaeus

(Based on Luke 19:1–10)

. . . he looked up and said to him, "Zacchaeus, come down immediately . . ." (Luke 19:5)

Zacchaeus was a scorned man. People laughed because he was short. They didn't like him because he cheated and hurt people. He longed to be a better person. Jesus showed him that the size of his body didn't matter; just the size of his heart. Kindergartners often feel lost in a world of tall people; help them rejoice that Jesus loves them just the way they are.

Music Center

Climb, Climb, Zacchaeus

Children will enjoy singing the old favorite, "Zacchaeus Was a Wee Little Man" or the song below.

(Tune: "Row, Row, Row Your Boat")

Climb, climb, Zacchaeus, climb, climb right up the tree.
There at the top you will surely find that Jesus you can see.

Look, look, Zacchaeus, look, look and you will see.
Here comes the crowd that's with Jesus, and He is walking
beneath your tree.

"Come, come, Zacchaeus, come, come down from your tree.
I'm going to your house, Zacchaeus, for lunch so you can be with Me."

Now, now, Zacchaeus, now, a better man you'll be.
Aren't you rejoicing that Jesus came by and saw you in your tree?

Nature Walk

Take a walk with the children, encouraging them to collect twigs, small branches, seeds, and leaves. Discuss safety rules about climbing trees with them. Display the children's objects along with books and pictures about trees.

Active Play Center

Playing Zacchaeus

Let the children pretend that a slide or jungle gym is a tree. They can go up when they hear "Here comes Jesus!" and down when they hear "Zacchaeus, you come down!"

Jesus Calls Zacchaeus

continued

When Zacchaeus Hid (Action Play)

Let the children make trees using building toys. Or they can do the action play below.

Zacchaeus climbs right up a tree (*Stand high; pretend to climb.*)
And gets way down inside. (*Scrunch down.*)
But Jesus loves him far too much (*Hug self.*)
To let Zacchaeus hide. (*Put hands up to cover face.*)
"Come down, Zacchaeus," Jesus says. (*Look up; motion with hand.*)
So Zacchaeus comes right down. (*Pretend to climb down.*)
And when the Lord goes to his house, (*Make "house" with hands.*)
He's the happiest man in town! (*Clap.*)

Art Center

A Tree for Zacchaeus

Materials needed: a large piece of newsprint to put on a wall, a large black felt marker, real leaves collected by the children in the summer or fall or copies of leaf on page 14, tape, brown and green poster paint, paintbrushes, paint smocks or other protectors

Directions: Paint a large outline of a tree trunk and branches on the newsprint. Lay this newsprint on the floor (over plastic or newspapers). Let the children add grass along the bottom edge of the newsprint by placing their hands in a shallow pan of green paint and then placing them on the paper. They can then either tape real or construction paper leaves on the tree branches, or paint "handprint" leaves there, as well. At the top, print "Jesus called to Zacchaeus." When dry, hang this on a wall. Tell this Bible story in front of it.

Snack Time

Serve cupcakes decorated with green gumdrops and milk. Or, serve a nice lunch for Jesus of grapes, apple slices, small slices of cheese and crackers, and lemonade.

Prayer: Thank You, dear God, for helping us be friends with Jesus. In Jesus' name, Amen.

Jesus Brings Easter Joy!

(Based on Matthew 27:45–28:11)

". . . tell his disciples: 'He has risen from the dead . . . '" (Matthew 28:7)

The awesome wonder of Easter is not in candy and colored eggs. It is in the realization that as tragic and, yet, necessary as Jesus' crucifixion was, it pales beside the thrill of His resurrection. Jesus is alive today, to love and help and lead us all. Share that thrill with the children.

Music Center

Children will enjoy tapes of triumphant Easter music, especially chimes or bells. Or sing "Praise Him, Praise Him, All Ye Little Children" or the songs below and on page 94. The children may accompany "O Easter Time!" and "Bells, Bells, Easter Bells" with jingle bells or other rhythm instruments.

Early in the Morning

(Tune: "Sweetly Sings the Donkey")

Early in the morning before the sun appears,
Here come some grieving women. Their eyes are full of tears.
They're at the tomb of Jesus. He's been their friend for years.
How sad! How sad! How very, very sad!
There is a mighty earthquake. The stone is rolled away.
The women see an angel! They don't know what to say.
The angel says, "He's risen! He is alive today!
Be glad! Be glad! Be very, very glad!"
That's why I love Easter. Come sing a song with me.
The Good News about Jesus we'll all share happily.
Jesus always loves us, and our best friend He'll be.
Be glad! Be glad! Be very, very glad!

O Easter Time!

(Tune: "O Christmas Tree!")

O Easter time! O Easter time!
I hear your church bells ringing.
O Easter time! O Easter time!
I hear your church bells ringing.
And what's the song your church bells say?
That Jesus is alive today!
O Easter time! O Easter time!
I hear your church bells ringing.

Jesus Brings Easter Joy!

continued

Bells, Bells, Easter Bells

(Tune: "Row, Row, Row Your Boat")

Bells, bells, Easter bells, ring out loud and clear!
Happily, happily, happily, happily, this glad time of year.

Bells, bells, Easter bells, Jesus died and then,
Happily, happily, happily, happily, Jesus rose again!

Nature Center

Display pots of spring flowers (such as tulips, lilies, crocuses) and seed packages. If possible, bring in a tame rabbit or caged canary. Discuss the wonders and beauties of spring with the children.

Playhouse and Blocks Centers

Materials needed: artificial flowers, baskets, dress-up clothes, lightweight foam or cardboard blocks or boxes

Directions: Help the children build the stone tomb. Then they can dress up as angels, guards, and Jesus' friends, bringing flowers and spices. For an earthquake, a hidden push can knock the tomb down.

Games Center

The children will enjoy puzzles about Easter time (Scriptural only) and spring. They could also build small roads for toy cars to drive to church on on Easter Sunday.

Active Play Center

Mary at the Tomb (Action Play)

Here comes Mary to the tomb. Her steps are very slow. (*Walk very slowly; look sad.*)
Why did Jesus have to die? He was her friend, you know. (*Pretend to weep.*)
Look! The tomb is open! There's an angel shining bright! (*Point; look surprised.*)
"Don't be afraid," the angel says. "Jesus is all right. (*Smile; reach out hands.*)
He died, but He's alive again. He rose right from the dead!" (*Sit with eyes closed, then jump up.*)

Mary isn't crying now. She's filled with joy instead! (*Smile; clap.*)

Going to the Tomb

Have the children walk as slowly as possible from "home" to the "tomb." Then after everyone repeats "Jesus is alive again," they can run back "home."

Jesus Brings Easter Joy!

continued

He Is Risen!

Form two teams. Place a "disciple" at two points. The first child, "Mary," on each team runs from the first "disciple" point to the second one and says, "He is risen!" The child then runs back. The second child on each team does the same, and so on. The first team to finish wins.

Art Center

The Empty Tomb

Materials needed: one copy of page 96 per child, pencil, crayons (optional: small flower stickers or glitter and glue)

Directions: Have the children complete their dot-to-dot pictures of the tomb opening. Then they can color their pictures, and fold on the dotted lines. (Optional: The children can add flower stickers or glitter to the angel, sunlight, and tomb.)

Easter Surprise to Share

Materials needed: two plastic egg shapes of any color with removable tops per child; two copies per child of the featured Bible verse for this story, written on strips of paper; Scriptural Easter stickers, soft jellybeans, or other small Easter candy

Directions: Let each child fill two egg containers with a folded-up Bible verse and candy, stickers, etc. Each child may have one and share the other.

Snack Time

Make peanut butter and jelly sandwiches, cut off the crusts, and then cut off the four corners on each to create a cross. Place the leftover corners around the plate for decorations. Serve with small pieces of fresh or canned fruit and milk.

Prayer: Thank You, dear God, for raising Jesus from the dead. We are so glad for Jesus! In Jesus' name, Amen.

Jesus Brings Easter Joy!

continued

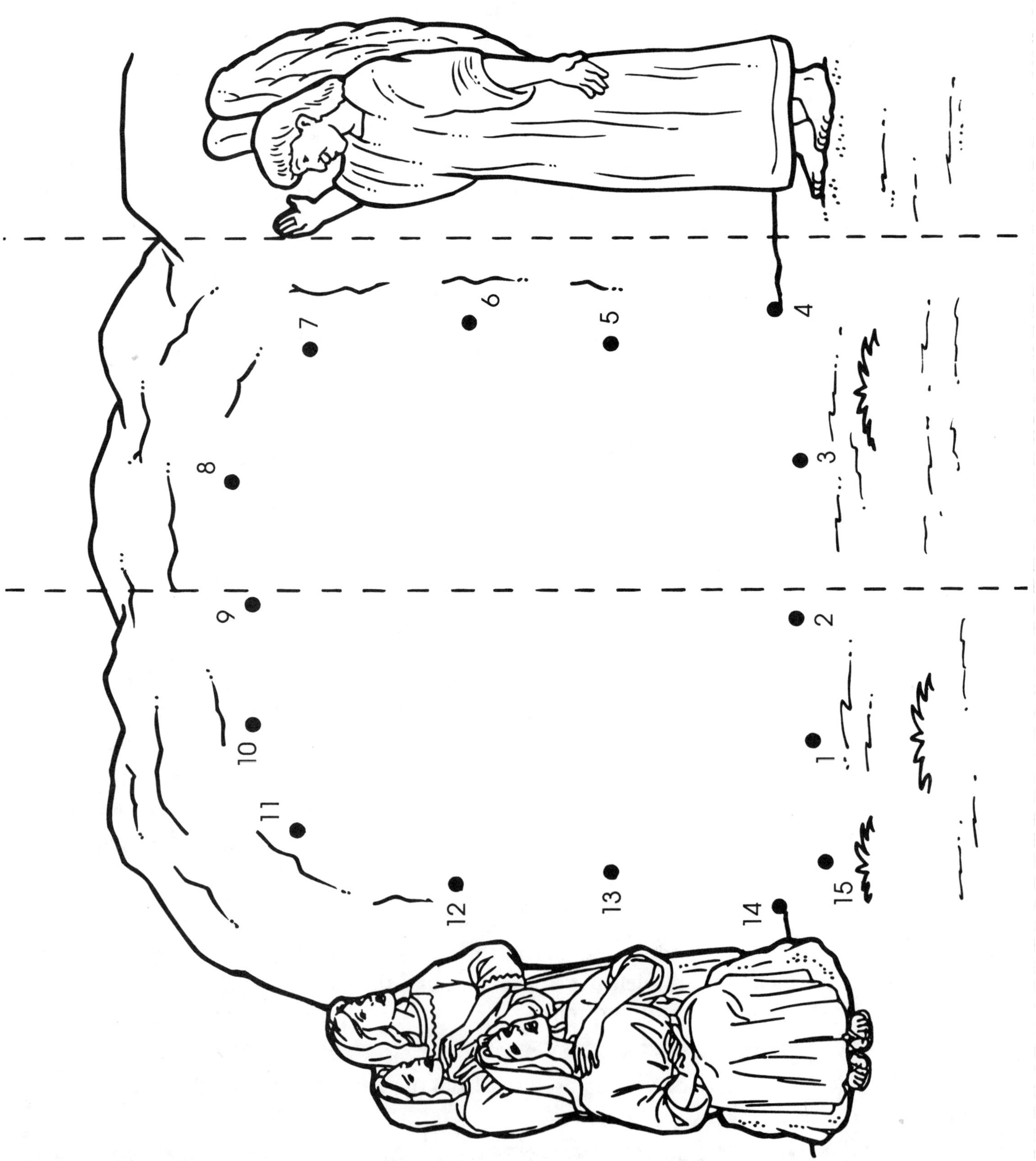